Practice What You Preach

Practice What You Preach

Teacher Accountability and Personal Values

Nicole Philp

ROWMAN & LITTLEFIELD
Lanham • Boulder • New York • London

Published by Rowman & Littlefield
An imprint of The Rowman & Littlefield Publishing Group, Inc.
4501 Forbes Boulevard, Suite 200, Lanham, Maryland 20706
www.rowman.com
86-90 Paul Street, London EC2A 4NE, United Kingdom

Copyright © 2022 by Nicole Philp

All rights reserved. No part of this book may be reproduced in any form or by any electronic or mechanical means, including information storage and retrieval systems, without written permission from the publisher, except by a reviewer who may quote passages in a review.

British Library Cataloguing in Publication Information Available

Library of Congress Cataloging-in-Publication Data
Names: Philp, Nicole, 1981– author.
Title: Practice what you preach : teacher accountability and personal values / Nicole Philp.
Description: Lanham : Rowman & Littlefield, [2022] | Includes bibliographical references. | Summary: "Practice What You Preach: Teacher Accountability and Personal Values helps teachers determine what values are of most importance to preach in the classroom as well as provides practical strategies for putting those values into practice"—Provided by publisher.
Identifiers: LCCN 2022014066 (print) | LCCN 2022014067 (ebook) | ISBN 9781475867749 (cloth) | ISBN 9781475867756 (paperback) | ISBN 9781475867763 (epub)
Subjects: LCSH: Moral education. | Affective education. | Teaching—Moral and ethical aspects. | Teachers—Attitudes. | Values clarification. | Educational accountability.
Classification: LCC LC268 .P475 2022 (print) | LCC LC268 (ebook) | DDC 370.11/4—dc23/eng/20220617
LC record available at https://lccn.loc.gov/2022014066
LC ebook record available at https://lccn.loc.gov/2022014067

For Dave, Marcail, and Caleb; I am blessed.
For my parents; my first teachers.
For my students; you are my joy.

Contents

Preface	ix
Introduction: "For They Preach, but They Do Not Practice"	xiii
Chapter 1: Train up a Child	1
Chapter 2: Fall and Rise Again	9
Chapter 3: Teach Yourself	23
Chapter 4: Sharpen Each Other	33
Chapter 5: Let Nature Teach You	45
Chapter 6: Turning Suffering to Hope	53
Chapter 7: Teach You Again	61
Chapter 8: A Model of Good Works	69
Chapter 9: Honor Everyone	81
Chapter 10: For the Rights of All	91
Chapter 11: Love Your Neighbor	101
Chapter 12: When We Stumble	111
Chapter 13: Faith, Hope, and Love	117
Chapter 14: Review and final exam	131
Bibliography	139
Acknowledgments	141
About the Author	143

Preface

As teachers, we have probably all chuckled over antiquated pictures of late-19th and early-20th century posters that displayed rules dictating a teacher's conduct. While we now laugh at the absurdity of the regulations that used to govern everything a teacher did, including keeping the chimney clean, not loitering in ice cream parlours, and how often and when it is appropriate to court (never if you are a female), those rules clearly reflected societal norms and expectations at the time.

Although I would certainly balk at signing a contract where I was told how many petticoats to wear and with whom I am allowed to ride in a vehicle, reflecting on these outdated lists has caused me to wonder . . . what are the expectations of teachers *now*? What would a similar set of rules look like for teachers in the 21st century?

Teachers may no longer have lists or rules that dictate their social lives and behavior, but they do have ethical codes of conduct to which they must adhere. These current professional codes of conduct tend to be less explicit than the old, prescribed lists, and expect educators to "maintain the honor and dignity of the profession," for example, rather than specifying *exactly* how that should be done.

Although "maintaining the honor and dignity of the profession" is a lofty goal to which educators should unarguably aspire, codes like this are so nebulous that they leave room for various interpretations. It is these differing interpretations that can result in a lack of teacher accountability, and that lack of accountability has repercussions for those who are most deserving of the best a teacher has to offer: the students.

A teacher who shows up to work on time, tends to their lessons, diligently completes their marking, and leaves the school at the ringing of the bell having completed the basic necessities of their job, can rightfully say they are "maintaining the honor and dignity of the profession." But is that enough? Is doing the bare minimum in *any* job, but *especially* in a career where modeling apathy and indifference towards education has the negative potential to influence a generation of children to do the same, acceptable?

When education systems not only fail to expect and encourage excellence from teachers, but also protect the rights of teachers who do the minimum expected of them, the results are predictable. The education profession becomes appealing to people who seek the adequate pay, good benefits, and fantastic holidays rather than attracting teachers who desire to make a difference in the lives of children. This lack of expectation and failure to encourage excellence affects more than just the recruitment of committed educators, it also makes it easy for veteran teachers to fall into habits of complacency, rather than challenging them to continually improve their practice.

Ironically, there is no vocation that matters more in shaping the future of our society, yet there are few, if any, career fields that expect less of its professionals.

I am not implying that we should revert to the early 20th century way of doing business by prescribing a list of actions to which teachers must attend. I am, however, advocating for more accountability in our school systems; accountability that must first begin with us, the educators.

While we may no longer need, nor do we want, the seemingly inappropriate and absurd list of teacher responsibilities that were common a century ago, perhaps it is not so inappropriate or absurd to still maintain expectations of those who are responsible for molding and educating our youth. When teachers hold themselves accountable to the pursuit of excellence in their professional lives and daily model accountability to personal values within their classroom, they implicitly teach students to do the same.

Practice What You Preach: Teacher Accountability and Personal Values explores how teachers can expect excellence from their students by first modeling it themselves. Each chapter focuses on a different value that can be "preached" and "practiced" in the classroom, supported with real-life anecdotes and practical strategies for implementation. Unlike the old lists of teacher duties, these chapter topics are not an exhaustive list of values that teachers *must* practice in their classrooms, but they are suggestions for how to hold your students accountable for their learning by first holding yourself accountable for your teaching.

The rewards for teaching with a "practice what you preach" philosophy are endless for both the students in your classroom and for yourself. When students see you personally living out the expectations you have for them, and holding yourself to the high standard to which you encourage them to strive to reach, they will respect you for your authenticity. Classroom discipline becomes minimal because students honor you and the effort you put into their lessons, and they value their time with you too much to interrupt it with disruptive behavior.

Through the foundation of honor and respect that you establish in your classroom by "practicing what you preach," you will also find students become unwilling to settle for less than what they know you expect; and more importantly, they will learn to be dissatisfied with settling for less than they know they can achieve. In that dissatisfaction with anything less than their own personal excellence, students also learn to have confidence, not just in their natural talents and skills, but in their ability to achieve their goals through hard work, grit, and perseverance.

Although we may not have a prescribed list of duties like our early 20th century educator counterparts, we would probably all like to subscribe to a list of rewards like those described above: classroom respect, minimal discipline, pursuit of excellence, and a love of learning. Achieving these goals in the classroom takes time, diligence, and intentional effort, but daunting though that might sound, rest assured that these rewards are achievable. Reaping these benefits is not dependent upon being fortunate enough to craft just the right lesson, stumble across the perfect classroom management strategy, or ascribe to the ideal educational philosophy. Rather, these types of rewards, for both you and your students, are dependent upon the one thing you can control: *you*.

When *you* decide which values are of utmost importance to hold as a standard in your classroom, and then hold *yourself* accountable to modeling those values, you will leave a legacy with students whose educational experiences will be about much more than curriculum. That experience will continue to serve them well beyond their years in your classroom and will help them develop into passionate, engaged, and contributing citizens of our communities.

It is relatively easy to deliver curriculum lessons to a group of students. But to do so in a manner that leaves a lasting legacy on the future citizens of our world requires much more than mere delivery. It requires you to "practice what you preach."

Introduction: "For They Preach, but They Do Not Practice"

> *"So do and observe whatever they tell you, but not the works they do. For they preach, but do not practice."*
>
> Matthew 23:3

Consider the teachers you know whom all students respect, all colleagues admire, and all parents desire to have as their child's educator. You can likely identify a list of attributes that make these teachers worthy of admiration and respect. Yet being able to identify that long list of great teaching characteristics will not guarantee a good teacher the height of greatness they seek in the classroom. The distinction between good teachers who do their job well and great teachers whose legacy lives on beyond the classroom is that the latter not only *believe* in the necessary characteristics of effective teachers, but also daily strive to put them into *action*.

In other words, the teachers who "preach, but do not practice" may be effective conveyers of content, but those educators who "practice what they preach" instruct lessons that go far beyond curriculum and have lasting implications for students' lives.

It is not just these teachers' adherence to curriculum that has earned them this level of esteem among students, colleagues, and parents, although they certainly attend to that with passion and enthusiasm. Rather, the elements that earn these educators the respect and admiration of students, colleagues, and parents is their commitment to providing children with the knowledge they will need to succeed in life, and most importantly, the understanding that these lessons are best learned through a lived model.

How does this distinction between teachers who merely convey content and those whose lessons have lasting implication on students' lives appear in the practical day-to-day routine of a classroom? To best understand this distinction, try to imagine yourself as a student in the classrooms of both types of teachers. First, consider the classroom practices of teachers who feel their job is merely to convey content; that is, teachers who "preach, but do not practice." These kinds of educators may very well be good teachers with exemplary lesson plans and admirable intentions, but their actions sometimes delegitimize what they say.

For example, students may hear such teachers talk gallantly about their love of education, but then skeptically question that passion when, day after day, they are shown videos in lieu of being engaged with well-planned lessons. Students may be encouraged by teachers to get involved in extra-curricular activities, but then ironically witness those same teachers rush out the door every day at 3:30. Students may also bear the grunt of teachers' exasperation when they fail to hand assignments in on time, but then are frustratingly forced to wait weeks to receive assessment feedback from the teachers who harped on them about meeting deadlines.

There is nothing "wrong" with these teachers who merely convey content. Their students will still be taught curriculum and will be given the information necessary to move on to the next level. What is "wrong" with this scenario, however, are the missed opportunities that can enrich students' learning when educators focus on content to the exclusion of everything else.

Educators who dedicate themselves to "practicing what they preach," on the other hand, recognize that the classroom provides opportunities to teach students in ways that can profoundly affect students' educational experiences. The students of teachers who "practice what they preach" witness educators turn daily *curriculum* instruction into life lessons on *integrity* simply through their actions.

"Preaching, but not practicing" was best illustrated through some examples of how students might perceive the hypocrisy of teachers saying one thing but then doing another. Likewise, understanding what "practicing what you preach" could look like in a classroom is best illustrated by considering specific examples, those of which can be gathered merely by surveying the students in one of these teachers' classrooms. As you read the following survey questions, consider how the students in your classroom would respond and then reflect on the sample student responses provided from a variety of classrooms where the teachers truly "practice what they preach."

- Is your teacher passionate about education? How do you know?

So passionate. Her mantra in math class—that we hear, like, every day—is that "math is beautiful." It's obvious she loves her job. She is always happy and gets super excited when she's teaching us new things. She even dresses up to get us interested in the concept, like when she dressed up as Batman

Introduction: "For They Preach, but They Do Not Practice" xv

to teach us about "super" power laws. Or when she came to class wearing a bedsheet as a toga to teach us about how the ancient Greeks discovered trigonometry. She tries to get us to enjoy math as much as she does.

- Do you get the feeling that your teacher respects you and enjoys having you in their class? What gives you that impression?

He does for sure. Every single class, Mr. H greets us at the door and shakes our hand as we enter the room. It's like he wants to personally welcome us to his class. It's pretty cool. I've never had a teacher do that before. And then during class, he calls us by name and somehow makes sure we all get a chance to offer our opinion.

- Does your teacher have high standards for you? What happens if you fail to meet those expectations?

Sometimes it's frustrating that we can't get away with slacking off in Mrs. T's class like we do in other teachers' classes. But I know we are lucky because she's trying to teach us to work hard so we can do our best. And as long as we prove we are working hard, she gives us all sorts of chances to do better. She just tells us we have to earn those chances. Which, when you think about it, makes sense.

- Does your teacher contribute to the overall sense of school spirit and involve the community in your learning? How?

Mrs. B comes dressed in the wackiest clothes every single time we have a dress up day at school. You can hear her yelling down the halls the day before a dress up day, reminding students to show their school spirit. Sometimes we laugh 'cause she's so over the top, but we all love it. She's the kind of person who is involved in everything. Not just in school, like with coaching and stuff, but also out in the community. Everyone knows and loves Mrs. B.

There are an infinite number of ways your students may answer those questions and each one would provide you with a clear reflection of how they see your classroom practices. Most significantly, however, is that students of teachers who "practice what they preach" will not only answer affirmatively to the first part of each question above, but they will also be able to provide specific examples to support that affirmation in response to the second part of each question.

When teachers do more than just disperse curriculum content but choose instead to actively live out their beliefs regarding what is of utmost importance in educating the whole child, not only can students definitively answer the above survey questions, but they also have positive leaders to follow, authority figures they can respect, and role-models worth emulating.

TIME IS OF THE ESSENCE

Besides their parents, teachers are the adults with whom children spend a huge portion of their time, approximately 14,040 hours, over the course of their developmental years. That number is only counting instructional time and does not include the hundreds of hours that children spend in the company of teachers for extra-curricular clubs, sports, and academic support. This is a humbling statistic that helps emphasize the amount of time with which teachers are gifted the opportunity to work with children. It is also a daunting statistic when considering the significance of the impact that much time allows teachers to have on the future generation of this world.

It is therefore a statistic that cannot be taken lightly.

ORIGIN OF "PRACTICE WHAT WE PREACH"

The old saying "practice what we preach," is probably the simplest way to describe the approach teachers need to take in their classrooms to make each one of those 14,040 (plus) hours count. There are other idioms that offer similar wisdom, such as "actions speak louder than words" and "walk the talk," but this particular phrase is profound in its wisdom, not only because of the appealing alliteration, but also because the words themselves have meaning that are worth further contemplation.

The phrase "practice what you preach" originates from the gospel of Matthew in the Bible and, depending on the translation, reads slightly different than how most people are accustomed to hearing it: "For they preach, but do not practice" (23:3). This verse is easier to comprehend when it is examined in its larger context:

> The scribes and the Pharisees sit on Moses' seat, so do and observe whatever they tell you, but not the works they do. *For they preach, but do not practice.* They tie up heavy burdens, hard to bear, and lay them on people's shoulders, but they themselves are not willing to move them with their finger. They do all their deeds to be seen by others. (Matthew 23:2–5)

In this more comprehensive look at the origin of the familiar phrase, Jesus is telling his followers to be critical of the religious leaders of the time. He points out that these leaders would rather burden their followers with the weight of labor and responsibility than do the work themselves or even help others who carry heavy burdens. And in the unlikely event that these leaders do take on some of the labor themselves, it is only so that they might be acknowledged and praised for it, rather than for the sake of doing good.

Jesus admonishes people to carefully observe the religious leaders and recognize that although their *words* may be of good character, their *actions* may prove otherwise.

Regardless of your religious beliefs or faith background, you can probably relate to the wisdom in these verses due to experiences you have had with people who are similar to those whom Jesus cautions against. How many colleagues have you worked with who "talk the talk" but do not "walk the walk"? How many politicians have you heard vow to serve the people whom they are elected to represent and then are exposed in the media for condemnable behavior? How many committee chairs have you noticed are quick to take the credit for a job well done, but fail to honor the work of those who made their success possible?

The hypocrisy of leaders who say one thing but do another has become so rampant in society that many people in positions of authority are now often regarded with skepticism; their followers almost anticipating them to falter.

Perhaps because this habit of failing to match actions to words is so prevalent that it has almost become acceptable, adults sometimes think they can expect kids to "do as I say, not as I do," whether it is parents in their households or teachers in their classrooms. Unfortunately, however, when adults attempt to do this, they are only contributing to a vicious cycle of developing cynical citizens who believe that no one will ever hold them accountable for their actions if their words are of good enough character, regardless of their behavior.

"For they preach, but they do not practice," may be common enough among in society, but classrooms should not be the training ground where children learn to do the same.

PURPOSE OF THIS BOOK

The goal of this book is to explore how teachers can "preach" what matters most in the classroom and then put those values into action. And what matters most is not always curriculum. (*Gasp*).

Curriculum content is important, so please do not misunderstand the intent of this statement; it is not to advocate for teachers to disregard the legal responsibilities they have to their profession. Rather the intent is to help teachers recognize that what is even more important than curriculum are the opportunities it provides educators to teach children the crucial lessons about life. And those lessons are best taught when they are modeled by teachers who diligently "practice what they preach."

It is in these moments, where school curriculum is intricately woven with life lessons, that teachers can "preach" about the things that are of utmost value; lessons like learning respect when studying characters' interactions in a novel; practicing collaboration and teamwork when engaging in a math competition; gaining an appreciation for stewardship of the earth through fieldtrips and explorations; and so much more. These values are then supported with real-life classroom antecdotes and practical examples of how they can be implemented into the daily routine of school life.

Like the biblical verse upon which the title of this book is based, each chapter opens with a verse that similarly presents a value that is worthy of investing your time and energy into as an educator, and worthy of being "practiced" through integrating them into curriculum lessons.

PRACTICE: NOUN, VERB, OR BOTH?

Because the "practice" part of the quotation is so important to the impact "practice what you preach" can have on a classroom full of students, that word itself bears further examination. The deliberate use of this word in this old phrase has two meanings, and therefore two implications for its lived-out reality in the classroom.

As a noun, the word "practice" means "the actual application or use of an idea, belief, or method, as opposed to theories relating to it" (Oxford University Press 2020). Whatever you decide is worthy of preaching must become an actual application in your classroom. Teachers cannot simply have a theory regarding these values and then hope that their students will come to live out these characteristics simply because they are theoretically embraced and talked about in the classroom. These values must be established routines that students come to expect and *respect* in their learning experiences.

As a verb, the word "practice" means to "perform (an activity) or exercise (a skill) repeatedly or regularly in order to improve or maintain one's proficiency" (Oxford University Press 2020). The implicit meaning in this definition has tremendous significance for the classroom; once you have determined the values that are worthy of preaching in your classroom, this definition encourages you to repeatedly and regularly perform them to improve your proficiency.

This definition of practice as a verb, however, does not mean that just because you might believe that stewardship of the earth is worthy of preaching that you must be an expert in renewable energy. Rather, practicing this belief means that you continue to work at the values you believe are crucial in life. As you practice to personally improve in living these values, you will also gain proficiency at instilling them in your classroom routines.

The best part of the word "practice" as a verb is that your students will witness your pursuit of these values as you put your beliefs into action. They will see for themselves that while perfection is not necessary, practice most definitely is.

Educators have the incredible opportunity to mold, shape, and influence the children who leave the classroom to become the future citizens of their communities. As such, there is no choice but to take that responsibility seriously and with honorable intent; and there is no better way to teach children than to be a living example of the most important lessons they can learn in school.

Determine what is worthy of "preaching," and then diligently, enthusiastically, and daily put those values into "practice." And then expect your students to do the same.

Chapter 1

Train up a Child

"Train up a child in the way he should go; even when he is old he will not depart from it."

Proverbs 22:6

"I really like Mrs. V," a nine-year old student commented about his teacher. "She's tough, but fair."

As a young student, this nine-year-old has already recognized a profound characteristic of effective teaching. When students describe their teachers as "tough, but fair," many other attributes are implicit in that simple phrase that can have lasting impacts on the students whose teachers put them into practice.

Students who see their teachers as "tough, but fair" recognize their teacher has high, but achievable, standards. Students who use this phrase are also indicating a mutual sense of respect for, and from, their teacher. This mutual respect comes from an awareness that despite being expected to work hard, students know their teacher is going to work equally as hard. Lastly, students who are taught by "tough, but fair" teachers are confident in the knowledge that although they may have to face consequences for mistakes, they will also have opportunities to learn from those errors.

Teachers who embody the "tough, but fair" philosophy that encompasses each one of these attributes are doing more than merely teaching children curriculum. These educators are training up children in ways that they will not depart from when they are older. The students of "tough, but fair" teachers will reap the benefits of those lessons when they graduate from high school and have the confidence to overcome obstacles, the assurance that they can learn from their mistakes without being defeated, and the certainty that they can earn success through hard work, all because they have already done so in their teacher's classroom.

The word "tough" can be construed as hard, cold, and unfeeling, which is not the characteristic to which good teachers aspire. Rather, effective teachers diligently practice the "tough love" that is warranted to get students to reach their own potential, or at the very least, to take that first step and recognize that they even have potential. Sadly, there are children sitting in desks in every classroom who not only fail to see their own value, but who also have such minimal self-confidence that they believe no amount of effort on their part will ever guarantee success, so why bother trying. This despondency, often misinterpreted and labeled as apathy, is heartbreaking.

Teachers have two choices in how to deal with kids in these situations. First, they can agree with these students in ways that both implicitly and explicitly confirm their assessment of themselves. Teachers can coddle these insecure kids, praise them for their mediocre effort, reward them for their mediocre performance and ultimately teach them to never expect more from themselves than mediocre results.

Alternatively, teachers can refuse to accept what they know should be unacceptable, and implicitly and explicitly teach these students to do the same. Rather than coddle them and praise their mediocre effort, teachers can challenge them and admire their deliberate effort when they rise to that challenge. Rather than reward them for their mediocre performance, teachers can establish assessment protocols that help students clearly see where they are currently achieving and provide them with the tools to improve. Rather than teach them to never expect more from themselves than mediocre results, teachers can show them what they are capable of, so they learn to never be satisfied with less.

When you know students are capable of more, *please* do not teach them to accept less from themselves by being the teacher who first accepts less from them. As philosopher John Stuart Mill said, "a pupil from whom nothing is ever demanded which he cannot do, never does all he can" (Mill 2019).

Educators need to expect, and *demand*, that kids push their limits and are challenged to work harder and do better than they think they can; otherwise, they will never understand the magnitude of their potential. This philosophy of expectation must be reflected in more than just refusing to let students take pride in handing in a pathetically written essay that was completed last-minute. This is a general philosophy that must permeate every nuance of the classroom, in the daily routine of assessment practices, through systems of rewards and consequences, and embedded in standards and expectations.

The mix of students who walk into the classroom arrive with varying degrees of natural ability and are all over the map in terms of motivation. There will be kids whose ingrained sense of determination will not let them quit, regardless of the difficulty of the task before them. There are other students who have had everything come easy for them, so when something presents a challenge, they prefer to give up than work hard to overcome it because they have never had to do so before, and usually do not know how. And then, of course, there are the children who fall in the middle, who have neither an overwhelming amount of talent nor the internal motivation to work toward the next step on the staircase of achievement.

All these students, regardless of where they fall on the continuum of ability and internal drive, need consistently high expectations and to be taught not to accept anything less than the best they have to give. The most successful kids are not necessarily the ones who have been gifted with natural ability but rather those who are intrinsically motivated to recognize their potential and work hard to reach it. Although this motivation to work hard seems to come more naturally for some kids, there is absolutely no doubt that every student can be trained to adopt perseverance and determination as part of their daily classroom routine if it is consistently *expected* of them and if they are *shown* what that looks like.

THE IMPORTANCE OF GRIT

Angela Duckworth is a psychology professor who has spent years researching the science of character development and published her findings in the book *Grit*. By studying and interviewing successful people in various professions, from NFL football players to musicians, Olympians to soldiers, she has concluded that regardless of the talent with which people are born, it is their "effort [that] counts twice" (Duckworth 2016, 42) in their pursuit for success.

She further describes talent and effort in a way that provides educators with a firm philosophical foundation for their classroom practice: "without effort, your talent is nothing more than unmet potential. Without effort, your skill is nothing more than what you could have done but did not" (Duckworth 2016, 51).

Upon leaving your classroom, do you want students reflecting on their time with you and recognizing what they did *not* do and did *not* accomplish because their best was *not* expected of them?

Not only should teachers apply this philosophy to the students in their classrooms, but they should also use it as a mirror to reflect on their own practices. At the end of the school year, are you satisfied with reflecting back on what you did *not* do and did *not* accomplish because you did *not* expect it of yourself?

Teachers must strive to meet their own potential as educators because failing to do so comes at the expense of their students' educational experiences.

When you can look back at your school year and honestly say that you have no regrets, that you offered your best to every student in your class, then it is very likely your students will have similar reflections. Students are much more likely to achieve their potential when their teacher not only expects that of them, but models that in their own professional routines. If students walk away with little else after they finish high school other than the ability to push themselves to never settle for less, they are guaranteed to be on the path to success.

You might argue there are many other important lessons students should be learning when they walk out the school doors for the last time, and you would not be wrong. Schools should teach students to become proficient readers and communicators, with a solid grasp of language skills that allow them to successfully communicate in whatever format will be required of them in their future careers. Students should also learn to be adept and skilled mathematicians who can do more than just memorize formulas and apply them but can also critically examine challenges and identify the patterns necessary to solve problems.

But while all that academic knowledge is worth striving for, it will be of little value if students do not also learn the perseverance, determination, and *grit* that Angela Duckworth's research has found to be the single most influential characteristic in determining success. Teachers cannot teach kids about grit, about how to continue to work hard even when the work gets harder, if they are not given the opportunity to fall as they climb toward their potential.

TEACHING GRIT: CLIMBING WALL METAPHOR

There are endless books written on the topic of how to teach kids not to be extrinsically motivated; that the tangible rewards for hard work should not be the reason they rise to a challenge. Rather, the motivation for success should come from within; the incomparable feeling of satisfaction when you have accomplished something you set out to do. This concept of intrinsic versus extrinsic motivation has been reframed in many professional development sessions as "grit" or "growth mindset."

Some people may be born with a more deep-rooted sense of intrinsic motivation and find it easy to challenge themselves and follow through with more difficult tasks for their own sake rather than for the extrinsic rewards so often offered for any level of success. But rest assured that although your students may not be "born" with this natural tendency to challenge themselves, it can most certainly be taught. Even more reassuringly, the secret to teaching intrinsic motivation (or "grit" or "growth mindset") is not some convoluted process or intricate strategy. Rather, intrinsic motivation can be taught by simply and repeatedly *expecting* it.

When the teacher's constant refrain in the classroom is that giving up is unacceptable, quitting is intolerable, and choosing not to strive for excellence is inexcusable, students inevitably learn to adopt those same philosophies. Through constant encouragement and support, students can learn through their academic lessons the effective life habits of not giving up, not quitting, and how to push themselves to strive for excellence.

Consider the teaching of "grit," "growth mindset," or "intrinsic motivation" as the process of learning the sport of wall-climbing. Using scaffolded instructional activities in the classroom as students learn new concepts is similar to the wall-climbing footholds that, on the beginner walls, are close together, prominently jutting out from the wall, easy to reach, and easy to hold on to. Those first footholds are barely off the ground, and like the relatively simplistic first tasks teachers give students to ensure their grasp of new material, are quick and easy to accomplish, the rewards instantaneous and momentarily satisfying. Students can look back and take pride in the fact that they are, indeed, climbing, but also be motivated when they look up and see how far they have left to go.

As students move up the wall, or delve into more complicated concepts, they must necessarily proceed with more caution. The rewards are not as instantaneous because as the wall steepens and the work gets harder, it takes more time to plan the next step on the move upward. Yet each challenging inch of upward movement is all the more satisfying for the achievement when students can look behind and recognize the progress they have made, and look ahead to see the lessening gap between themselves and the top of the wall.

Sometimes students will run out of strength and when they release the tenuous grip of their fingers on a rock, it is parallel to admitting they have gone as far as they can on their own and need assistance to master the next concept. With their feet firmly back on the bottom, they can study the wall with their teacher, reflect on where they missed a foothold (or which concept they did not understand), and work with their teacher to plan how to adjust their climbing strategy for success on the next attempt.

Regardless of the activity, be it intellectually challenging academic outcomes or wall climbing, however, there is only one way to get better. Practice.

When students take time to reflect and consider the results of having been challenged by their teacher to try the harder question, to tackle the more difficult concept, or to figuratively reach for that hold that was yet above their head, they will be able to see the evidence of their strength increasing. They may never seek to complete the challenging questions, nor would they have the ability to do so, if they did not have their teacher on the ground level, encouraging them to build their capacity for overcoming obstacles every step of the way.

The further they climb, the easier it could be for students to say, "I have gone far enough," let go, and enjoy the swing on the way back down. But as time goes on, the goal is for the opposite to become true. The higher students climb, and the closer they get to achieving the top of the wall, the more difficult it should be for them to hear their teacher's repetitive mantra of "seeking the intrinsic reward" and, as is the deliberate intent right from the beginning, the more internal that motivation will become.

By the time students finish a class with a teacher who embraces this consistent expectation of striving for the intrinsic reward, they are likely no longer looking over their shoulders to make sure their teacher is observing and admiring their progress on the scaffolded conceptual assignments. Rather, they are likely too intent on achieving personal satisfaction from tackling the challenging tasks, and reaching for that next handhold, to be concerned about making sure their teacher witnesses their triumph so they can earn a reward.

Perhaps the best part of this metaphor, however, is not the visual image it provides of the climber slowly gaining strength and ability to separate themselves from the easy and achievable first steps off the ground level.

It is the image of the supporter on the ground.

For compliant students, the beginning of the climb is usually for the teacher, the "good student" in them wanting the teacher's approval when they do what is asked of them. As they continue the slow climb on their journey towards truly understanding and embracing this concept of seeking the "intrinsic reward" in their work, they will know without a doubt that they can always look back and see their teacher observing their progress and can hear that teacher's encouragement in their ear. The higher they climb, however, the more distance they put between themselves and the teacher's ability to observe and encourage them. And the climb becomes their own.

Regardless of how high they climb, how much ground they gain on their journey to fully developing their own sense of intrinsic motivation, students will know, without needing to see, that their teacher never once let go of the supporting rope. The rope, and that steadfast presence, keeps them safely tethered to the ground.

This is what teaching grit looks like. Kids need to be mentored and shown how to climb with their teacher's constant support, deliberate repetition, and continuous challenges . . . until they are ready to go the distance on their own. Although the role of a mentor is, in theory, to make themselves dispensable in the sense that the ultimate goal is to ensure kids can become independent life-long learners, while they are on this journey toward intrinsic motivation, the teacher can never walk away.

As long as they are with you and in your care, students need your classroom to be the safety net should they fall, and they need to know that you are there to catch them when they do. Not to coddle them, mind you, and falsely reassure them that they *did not* fall, but rather to acknowledge their temporary lack of success as an inevitable obstacle on the climb to personal achievement that they can choose to overcome.

TRAIN UP A CHILD

Expect the best from your kids and through your classroom routines of teaching grit, you will also be training students to expect the best from themselves. Early childhood educator, Susan, runs a daycare out of her home and found that children are trainable from a young age. When Susan had to run an errand one afternoon, she asked a friend to help her out by watching the gaggle of children for a few hours. "After snack time," she informed her friend, "do *not* take their plates and clean up after them. I have trained them to do that themselves."

Sure enough, this adorable group of one- to four-year-old children obediently (and with a lot giggling, because what else do you expect from a group that age?) took their plates to the sink when they finished their snack. The older ones even offered to help the younger ones to ensure that the task was done. Had Susan's friend stepped in to do the job for them, she would have undermined the work the Susan had done to get these young children to have confidence in doing this task for themselves.

If a childcare provider can train her little ones to meet her expectations, how can educators not also apply this same philosophy to the students in the classroom? Teachers have the unique opportunity to use their classrooms as a training ground to not only teach students to meet our expectations for them, but also to train them to set similarly high expectations for themselves. When this is done consistently, without stepping in to undermine the confidence students gain by doing the work themselves, they will leave the classroom with the desire to never settle for less than they know they have to give.

Chapter 2

Fall and Rise Again

"For the righteous falls seven times and rises again."

Proverbs 24:16

A psychiatrist renown for her "Ruthless Compassion Institute," Dr. Marci Sirota commented on this topic of falling and rising again on a radio interview one afternoon: "There is a difference between leniency and kindness," she said. "We do not want to raise little narcissists who have not learned the value of hard work. But finding the balance means allowing them a kind place to fall when they fail. We need to apply rigor and discipline in our classrooms, tempered with compassion and kindness."

The lack of rigor and discipline that has resulted in the "everyone deserves a ribbon" philosophy that has become so prevalent in education is concerning. Children are being educated in a system where it seems consequences are few and far between for inappropriate behavior, where rewards are dispersed for the tiniest bit, or even lack, of effort, and where truly hard-working, deserving students go unrecognized because that recognition might offend someone else.

As a result, this generation of children is growing up into adults who have been led astray by being taught that they deserve jobs and salaries simply because they exist. They are learning, the hard way and in a world that does not suffer fools or laziness very well, that showing up late, failing to complete tasks, and poor performance does not actually "make the grade" in the real world like it did in school. If this is how children are being "trained up" in schools today, what does that suggest for their future?

Educators hear so often about the necessity of preparing students for the "real world" with communication skills, critical thinking, and the ability to work collaboratively. Teacher professional development workshops are often focused on these attributes, and rightly so. These skills should be modeled and expected in schools, but the expectations of the real world go beyond students' abilities to work well with others. Teachers also need to model how, and expect students to, work hard, persevere, and develop tenacity. And what is probably even more important, the classroom experience needs to teach kids to have faith that these characteristics are all that is required to reach their potential.

Unfortunately, many education systems have embraced practices that teach students habits of complacency that are the polar opposite of the characteristics of success that psychologist and author Angela Duckworth has discovered in her work with "gritty" people, which were explored in chapter 1.

CONSEQUENCES OF PREVENTING THE FALL

There is huge potential in the power of failure, but unfortunately this belief goes against the grain of many current educational theories and trends today. Despite the theory that seems to say otherwise, however, in the real experience of working with kids on a daily basis, it quickly becomes apparent that students cannot learn how to dig deep, pull themselves up, dust themselves off, and try again, if their mistakes are discounted and they are rewarded regardless of their questionable achievement.

Students cannot learn that real life will not give them gifts if their education system continues to wrap up their marks in pretty packages and find ways for everyone to be equally successful, regardless of whether that success was rightfully earned. These gifts are cleverly disguised with edu-jargon that deludes teachers, administrators, and parents alike, into thinking someone smarter than they are has invented the best way to teach, when perhaps that is not the case.

Some well-educated theorists have long been out of a classroom, and have rarely, if ever, had the opportunity to actually put into practice the philosophies they preach. While well intentioned, these trendy educational-fad experts should not make good teachers, administrators, and parents question what they know is practical and best for kids.

For example, practices like "social promotion" (i.e., no-failure policies) are touted as being implemented in the best interests of a child's mental health because of the belief that kids will give up on themselves and quit school altogether if they are held back from advancing to the next grade with their age-like peers. Social promotion advocates believe that moving students on to the next grade avoids the "social and emotional devastat[ion] and . . . increased personal, behavioral, and academic problems" (Zwaagstra, Clifton and Long 2010, 147) that are inevitable with holding students back to repeat a failed grade.

That sounds compassionate and reasonable in *theory*, but the *reality* of this type of philosophy is not nearly so warm and fuzzy. Whether they are given credit for it or not, kids are smart. And many of the astute, and yet apathetic, children in classrooms are very quick to pick up on the fact that they cannot fail regardless of their performance (or lack thereof). If parents are not invested enough in their children's education to ensure that they are meeting the requirements of their grade, these kids can choose to do next to nothing, or even *do nothing*, and get "compassionately" passed on to the next grade level without having learned the prerequisite skills required to be successful.

This practice of social promotion is merely a symptom that is indicative of a larger concern facing education: the lack of accountability. When education systems adopt the philosophies that students should not be held responsible for their work, that consequences should not be imposed when students fail to meet a standard, and that standards themselves are discriminatory, the consequences for education systems, for youth, and therefore for the future of society, are staggering.

Consequence 1: Lack of skills

By the time elementary students, who have been educated with the type of philosophy that does not hold them accountable for their learning, reach high school where credits and grades matter for post-secondary applications, some of them do not have the ability to achieve success due to their lack of sufficient academic skills and ineffective work habits.

High school math teachers have noted this lack of skills when concepts such as factoring quadratic equations have evolved from being considered a basic concept in past curricula to something most kids currently struggle to understand, simply because they have never been expected to know their multiplication facts.

A university English professor noted that she used to hold extra seminars for students who wanted to delve deeper into poetry or explore the rich nuances of an author's language. Now, she comments that her extra seminars are on sentence structure and basic grammar skills because the students who enter her class from high school do not have that foundational knowledge required to succeed at the post-secondary level.

Ironically, education systems that proudly claim not to "fail" students, are failing them anyway, when they do not expect students to learn the basics in school, nor hold them accountable for that learning.

Consequence 2: Classrooms become a melting pot of abilities

While the melting pot of abilities in a classroom has always been true in education, as no age-like group of children will ever be homogenous, the philosophy of not holding students responsible for their learning has exacerbated this truth to extreme measures. Children who struggle to learn how to read, but could be taught and pushed to read at least slightly below grade level, are often several grades below because no one holds them accountable for achieving their potential.

As a result, teachers find themselves facing the impossible and unrealistic task of trying to catch every student up to grade level, meanwhile also feeling burdened to advance those who are prepared for additional challenges. It is a situation that is good for *no one*—not the children who are so far behind that they feel they will never catch up, not the children who are roughly at grade level and get forgotten in the mix because teachers' efforts are focused on the multitude of children who are not yet at grade level, not the kids who are bored in class because the learning pace has been deaccelerated to accommodate the lower-level kids, and certainly not the teacher who cannot possibly meet the needs of all of these kids.

Consequence 3: Curriculum necessarily gets watered down

When jurisdictions are faced, year after year, with students who are unable to successfully grasp the curriculum content at grade level, they are forced into the position of making accommodations, and tragically this often results in modifying the curriculum expectations.

Did kids get dumber over the years? Absolutely not. The system has just stopped expecting them to be as smart, or to work hard to achieve as much as their counterparts did a couple of decades ago. As long as schools abide by this philosophy, they will continue to "undermine the credibility of the public education system" (Zwaagstra, Clifton and Long 2010, 150), which should be both shameful to all educators and horrifying to all parents.

The example given earlier of students struggling to factor because they do not know their multiplication tables is also an example that supports this argument. Factoring quadratic equations, in some educational systems, used to be a concept taught to 13-year-olds in middle school. Recognizing that students at this age are not capable of applying the multiplication skills they do not have to achieve this concept, the education "gurus" responsible for curriculum in this system removed this concept from middle years' math education and reserved it for high school students. Even then, senior students can be observed pulling out their calculators to determine two numbers that multiply to 24.

Watering down the curriculum serves no one's best interests. By doing so, students are no longer being taught the difficult concepts in public school. Instead they are essentially being taught that they are not capable of achieving those difficult concepts. When they get to post-secondary, they quickly realize how deficient their skills are and then have no one to blame but the system that, again, failed them by not ensuring they are prepared with the knowledge and work ethic required to be successful.

Consequence 4: Coddle minimum effort

Kids' lack of success over the years, due to the fact that they knew there was no consequence for poor performance, has inspired the development of many other practices and policies to support the "no-accountability" philosophy. An example of this is the endless number of assessment rewrite opportunities that are now an accepted and expected practice in many schools. The premise of the rewrite philosophy is that all students should be able to achieve the highest level on every outcome and that they deserve as many opportunities as necessary to reach that goal. Again, like social promotion, this does not sound like a terrible idea in theory. But, as with social promotion, kids prove their intelligence by abusing this philosophy.

Rather than work hard, study harder, and prepare to do well on the first assessment, students are happy to do poorly on an assessment because they know they will be given as many opportunities to rewrite as it takes to get the desired achievement. They also know that with no consequence for poor performance, they can use that first attempt as an opportunity to get a sense of what is being assessed and prepare accordingly to be successful on their second, or third, or fourth . . . attempt.

This philosophy puts all the onus on teachers, forcing them to come up with various assessment opportunities, and then mark those various assessments, for students to rewrite until they are satisfied with their marks. Many teachers have given up on that extra work and have simply adopted the practice of allowing their students to rewrite the exact same assessment over, and over, and over . . . until they get their desired level of achievement.

What do students learn from this type of assessment practice? The concepts of the unit? That is unlikely when they are just memorizing the questions and the right answers from the assessment so they can do better the next time. Do these types of practices teach students to take responsibility for their own learning? Obviously not when the teacher is the one assigned all the work of having to create (if they so choose) new assessments and then mark them. So what do these types of rewrite assessment practices teach students?

This expectation of countless unearned opportunities to improve their mark is teaching children to expect the same when they graduate; that they will not have to learn from, or fix, their mistakes but rather will be given an infinite number of do-overs. These unearned rewrite assessment practices are teaching kids they are entitled to the easy way out, that if they do not feel like putting in the work, they will still be handed repeated opportunities to succeed. Allowing students to repeatedly rewrite, without having *earned* that privilege, teaches them they will never be held accountable for their own performance.

These are dangerous lessons with which to send young adults out into the world.

Consequence 5: Increased anxiety

In the earlier years and even into middle school, some students find it almost comical how easy it is to "pass." Yet as the years go on and they recognize they are falling further and further behind their peers because they have simply never bothered to acquire, nor been held responsible for acquiring, the necessary academic skills, these same kids who may have initially enjoyed the free ride soon become riddled with anxiety. As the end of high school approaches, they come to understand that future failure is almost inevitable because they know they cannot do the work.

Behavior issues, which often escalate in middle years anyway as kids test their boundaries, tend to evolve into absenteeism and truancy. The three-year graduation rate that many education systems hold as a goal for all high school students very quickly seems unachievable for these kids who not only lack the academic skills they need to be successful, but neither do they have the confidence gained from having overcome past hurdles to apply to future challenging situations.

Mental health is currently one of the most targeted areas of focus in schools and workplaces. While failing kids is purported as a philosophy designed to protect the mental health of children, ironically it is having the opposite effect. Not allowing students to *experience* failure might give them a temporary illusion of confidence and success. But that illusion is one that will quickly be dispelled in the long term when obstacles arise that they do not know how to overcome. On the other hand, when students are expected, *and taught how*, to rise again when they fall, their mental resilience will gradually strengthen to the point where they can endure even the most challenging of obstacles.

The truth is, kids do not have to fail for accountability policies to work. They just have to know they could, and that they will be held responsible for their learning. Prior to the era of social promotion, parents and students were much more diligent about ensuring assignments were completed to at least a minimum standard of expectation. Teachers were more likely to communicate with parents because when work was incomplete, students faced the possibility of being held back.

Not necessarily failing kids, but allowing them to know that is a possibility, provides the motivation required for them to simply do the work. And when that motivation becomes habitual, it evolves from being an extrinsic factor to being internalized as necessary on the path to success. As a result, students learn the skills they need to be successful at the next grade level, the classroom's mixture of abilities is a more even playing field, the curriculum can be written to challenge students, assessment policies can hold students accountable rather than coddle them, and perhaps most importantly, students develop an innate sense of pride in their accomplishments and confidence in their abilities to succeed.

Embrace the Gray Area

Lest the previous examples are perceived as arguments to oppose giving children second chances and having compassion for kids who struggle, it should be clarified that is not, indeed, the purpose of presenting these points. Absolutes as far as any educational philosophy goes will never meet children's needs, whether it is the "old" philosophies of pass/fail or the "new" philosophies of ensuring everyone achieves a high level of success.

The only philosophy that will meet students' needs is recognizing that absolutely each and every child deserves a quality education that will challenge, inspire, and teach them to be successful and contributing members of society.

This belief means that not every child who fails to meet the curriculum criteria for their grade level should necessarily fail that grade. Nor should every child be socially promoted regardless of their academic performance. These decisions are the epitome of a "gray area," a gray area that cannot be avoided because it is messy, but one that needs to be embraced for the sake of the kids in every classroom. This cannot be an absolute philosophy, nor should it be a black and white policy written in stone in the graveyard of decimated educational philosophies.

PUT PREACHING INTO PRACTICE: TEACHING KIDS TO RISE AGAIN

Rather than see educational practices as a dichotomy, where teachers must choose to either coddle kids by not holding them accountable or to employ the old "spare the rod, spoil the child" philosophy, the real power in helping students be successful is in finding a balance between the two.

There are ways to work within the system to compassionately hold students accountable and to teach them that when they get knocked down seven times, they should get up eight. Even more importantly in that metaphor, teachers need to allow the consequences of students' actions to knock them down; and rather than picking them up, educators need to establish routines that teach students how to get back up on their own so that the next time they fall, it will not be so painful.

The last thing education systems should be doing is cushioning kids' falls so that the soft landing gives them the illusion that it is acceptable to stay down and revel in the comfort of mediocrity rather than doing the hard thing of rising and trying again to accomplish the goal they had originally set for themselves.

The previous criticism of the "no accountability" philosophy and its consequences would be hypocritical if all that was provided was countering theoretical arguments. As with most educational philosophies, it is not helpful to preach about a theory without providing concrete tools to put that philosophy into practice.

What follows are two examples of routines that have been established for language arts and math classes and were designed with this "fall down and get back up" philosophy in mind. While no routine or set of procedures is ever foolproof, these ideas have been successful in getting students to be accountable for their own work. These classroom policies have alleviated a lot of stress of having to chase kids to get their work done and eliminated some phone calls home because, according to students, these expectations are "tough but fair."

The "Responsibility Rules" for language arts courses in Table 2.1 are an effort to honor Dr. Sirota's suggestions to temper "rigor and discipline" with "compassion and kindness." These rules are an effective blend between the desire to firmly hold students accountable as well as the recognition that students need the opportunity to redeem themselves when they have made mistakes; after all, would teachers not want the same when they err in their professional lives?

When students fail an exam, or even get a passing mark with which they are dissatisfied, they should not be refused the opportunity to improve if they are willing to continue learning and advance their understanding. What is critical, however, is that students *earn* that opportunity for redemption. Second, third, and fourth chances cannot come for free, otherwise they will be expected, taken for granted, and completely devalued. A similar practice in a mathematics class is described in Table 2.2.

These "Responsibility Rules" and expectation of academic rigor discourages students from coming to class unprepared to write the test, getting a sense of what they need to know, and expecting a free second chance if they are unsuccessful. Expecting students to complete the practice questions and attend extra math help sessions to earn their second chances teaches kids to

Table 2.1. Responsibility Rules: Language Arts

- For any written assignment, you will be offered two due dates.
  - **Due Date 1: Feedback**
    The first due date is optional and is an opportunity for you to receive feedback on your draft. You will then have time to ask questions, edit, and revise your draft before submitting it for the second due date.
  - **Due Date 2: It is DUE**
    The second due date is non-negotiable. You must hand in your work by this date to receive a mark for this outcome.

- *What happens if I miss Due Date 1?*
  - Nothing, except that you have missed out on the opportunity to get thorough, quality feedback from an expert (your teacher!) in the field on this assignment.
  - Nothing, except that you did not take advantage of a free opportunity to improve your mark on this assignment.
  - Nothing, except that you have missed the opportunity to improve your skills as a writer and grow as a student.
  - Honestly . . . why would you miss this due date?

- *What happens if I miss Due Date 2?*
  - You get a zero.
  - *GASP* . . . yes . . . a zero.

- *How do I make up for missing the due dates?*
  - You do not get a chance to make up for missing Due Date 1. That is a gift that you cannot earn back on this particular assignment, but hopefully you regret missing it and recognize the value in meeting Due Date 1 for the next assignment.
  - You can, however, recover from missing Due Date 2, but you have to **EARN** that opportunity. You and I will meet outside of class time to determine:
    1. Why you missed the due date in the first place.
    2. What support you require to complete the assignment.
    3. What additional learning opportunities you will have to complete to **EARN** a second chance to turn in your late assignment.
    4. A third due date that you **WILL NOT MISS**.

Table 2.2. Responsibility Rules: Mathematics

- **Prepare for success:** For every assessment you will be given advance notice and the opportunity to prepare for success.
  What does "prepare for success" look like in this class?
    - Authentic exploration of the concepts
    - Expert instruction
    - Practice questions with feedback
    - Math-help sessions offered outside of class time

- **Unit Assessment:** Each unit culminates in a review activity and some type of unit assessment. If you have taken advantage of the above "prepare for success" opportunities, you will likely do very well on this unit assessment.

    - *What if I "prepared for success," but wasn't successful?*
        - Don't worry.
        - In the event that there is a concept that you struggled to do well on despite your hard work, we will work together outside of class time to clarify your understanding. When you are prepared to do so, you will have the opportunity to rewrite that assessment and improve your mark.

    What if I didn't "prepare for success," and was successful?
    - Aren't you lucky?
    - You may have understood the concepts well enough to be successful on the unit assessment, but be aware that in missing out on some of the "prepare for success" learning opportunities, you have also missed out on pieces of the concept that may not have been covered on the unit assessment. In other words, you succeeded, but you also missed out on some learning.

    What if I didn't "prepare for success," and wasn't successful?
    - Shocking.
    - In order to **EARN** the opportunity to improve your mark, you will attend extra math-help sessions and complete every practice question that was assigned during the unit.
    - *Every question?* Yes, every question. Keep in mind that you had class time and math help sessions available to you throughout the entire unit to complete the practice.

value those opportunities in the first place and see them as a way to prepare for success, rather than as a punishment for not doing well.

Do these "Responsibility Rules" work? Not 100% of the time. However, in the lived experience of implementing these policies, very few students are unsuccessful, and the ones who do not pass the course are not surprised, angry, or think it is unfair. It is a failure they know they have earned and recognize they could have easily avoided had they only followed the expectations.

Lesson learned. More importantly; *life* lesson learned.

FAIR, CONSISTENT, AND COMPASSIONATE

Because of the important life lessons students can learn from classroom policies that expect responsibility, your students would be well-served if you would consider implementing your own set of accountability standards. In doing so, it is imperative to remember that you are working with children, young human beings whose lives bring all sorts of turmoil to the classroom that defy the logic of any system you try to implement. When your classroom accountability routines are *fair, consistent,* and *compassionate*, however, both you and your students will reap the rewards. But each one of those words is key in the success of implementing your own routines.

The expectations must be *fair*. Teachers cannot assign an essay, set the deadline in two days' time, and then start handing out zeroes when students miss the date. If teachers are going to implement a rigid standard regarding deadlines, then these deadlines must be realistic and achievable.

A good practice is to discuss possible deadlines with students to make sure they are practical. You may not be able to expect quality work handed in the day after the football home-opener, for example. Acknowledging their busy lives, especially as they relate to school events, shows students you respect their commitment to other activities and will work with them to find a reasonable balance. Allowing them the opportunity to "negotiate" the due date helps them own the responsibility for it and makes it difficult for them to argue later that it was unfair.

A typical routine established with the language arts "Responsibility Rules" is to set the editing due date for written tasks a week after the assignment is given and then give students one to three periods, depending on the assignment, within that week to work on the essay in class. Students who want to meet the editing deadline will have to do some work outside of class to get it completed in time.

Following the editing due date, students may get one more class period to work on their revisions so that the teacher is accessible to answer any questions they may have regarding the feedback they were given on their first draft; meanwhile the students who did not meet that first deadline get one more class period to write. The second due date is always set for a day or two after that. There are no surprises with this system and no student would be able to argue the expectations are unfair.

Expectations must also be *consistent*. Despite the fairness of the "Responsibility Rules," it is very effective for teachers to anticipate taking action when the first "real" due date rolls around. There will always be a couple of students in every class who either want to test your own adherence to the rules (not very common) or who simply do not believe they will be held accountable to such a rigid standard when it has never been expected of them before (much more common).

Unfortunately for these students, they become the example through which every other kid in the class learns that the teacher is serious about due dates and strict in their expectations of excellence. When you assign the first few zeroes to the one or two students who failed to take you seriously, you will rarely get an argument from those students. They simply *know*. They will very likely sheepishly admit to their error, apologize, and promise to do better the next time. And guess what? The majority inevitably do if your consistent expectations do not fluctuate.

With this type of consistent system in place, students will come to know what you expect, they will know the consequence if they fail to meet that expectation, and they can trust that you will follow through with imposing it if their behavior happens again. And students who choose to do the extra research, reading, or practice questions that is required of them to earn a second chance never fail to miss the next deadline because the amount of work they have had to do to earn it is not worth leaving that mark at a zero the second time around.

Lastly, despite the critical components of maintaining fairness and consistency when establishing routines, it is also imperative to temper rigid expectations with *compassion* when it is warranted. An example of a lived classroom experience perhaps best illustrates the necessity of compassion.

A dedicated student, Stuart arrived uncharacteristically late the morning a presentation was due, and he asked his teacher if he could present at a later date. Without providing a reason or excuse, his teacher had no choice but to firmly reply with the routine statement: "You know the drill. Presentations are due today. If you needed an extension, you had to ask before the morning it is due." He nodded, clearly expecting that to be the answer, and went and sat down in his desk until his name was called when it was his turn.

A typically above-average student, Stuart ended up doing a terrible job of his presentation and collapsed into his desk with his head down afterward, clearly defeated with what he correctly perceived to be a failed exhibition of his knowledge. What his teacher did not know, until after class when another student enlightened her, was that this poor kid had run over his pet dog of fifteen years prior to coming late to class that morning.

These types of experiences provide opportunities for teacher reflection. While it is imperative to hold the bar high and maintain rigid standards so students will always know what to expect, if a student like Stuart is unwilling to be honest about his situation, this indicates that he did not think his teacher would have compassion. In these situations, when the teacher realizes too late that consistency perhaps took too much precedence over compassion, all that can be done is to offer sympathy, kindness . . . and another chance.

Stuart's teacher went and found him out in the hallway where he was trying to choke back tears of grief for his pet and anguish over his miserable presentation. Empathizing with his loss, she sympathetically commented how she could not imagine the tragedy he had experienced that morning and assured him he would have the opportunity to present again at a later date when he was ready. His relief was palpable.

Rigid standards and high expectations are necessary and good, but only when implemented with kindness and compassion. Unfortunately, there is no prescription for how to know which situations in students' lives are worthy of you allowing some flexibility in your classroom routines. It is a gray area that every teacher needs to balance for themselves, one that you may find yourself reflecting on almost daily when a new situation arises to challenge the process that you believe in. But that is okay.

If teachers are not challenged to see things in different ways or challenged to find ways to hold kids accountable while also respecting the life stories they bring to the classroom, then they will never get better as educators.

Implementing these kinds of routines and expectations will develop a foundation of respect for the academic process in your classroom. The best part of staying true to these standards is that the word will get out in a school, and your reputation for being "tough, but fair" will precede you into the classroom. Students will walk into your classroom knowing what to expect and experience firsthand the truth of what they have heard on the day the first assignment is due.

In his book *What Great Teachers Do Differently*, Todd Whitaker comes to the conclusion that "great teachers focus on expectations. Other teachers focus on rules. The least effective teachers focus on the consequences of breaking the rules" (2013, p. 13). While it is necessary for students to face fair and consistent consequences when they break the rules, it is the expectations, not the consequences, that should be the focus of the classroom environment. When the expectation is for students to rise again when they have fallen, and you have provided a ladder on which they have support to climb from that fall, you will reap the rewards of motivated and confident students.

Even more significantly, your students will reap the rewards that can only be gained when they are intentionally taught to own their mistakes and learn from their failures.

Chapter 3

Teach Yourself

"You then who teach others, do you not teach yourself?"

Romans 2:21

The previous chapter was about expecting the best from kids with examples of how to hold students accountable for their own performance, thereby teaching them a sense of responsibility that they can take with them into the future. But there is a caveat in teaching students these life lessons and a necessary caution that will be presented in this chapter. No matter how rigid teachers are with their standards, how high they set the bar of expectation, or how supportive they are in encouraging students when they fail to meet these standards and expectations, all this work amounts to very little if teachers do not first expect the same of themselves.

If the goals of schooling are to teach students to *value education*, *work hard to achieve it*, and *develop a sense of grit* in the face of adversity, as the adults in the classroom and the experts in education, teachers need to first "teach themselves" what that looks like. Educators cannot hypocritically teach their students to achieve their best if they are unwilling to hold themselves to that same standard. Todd Whitaker (2013) believes that "accepting responsibility is an essential difference between more effective and less effective employers, teachers, principals—even parents [and that] . . . success in any profession starts with a focus on self" (40–41).

The children in your classroom cannot be expected to accept responsibility for the role they play in their own learning if you do not first accept, and model, responsibility for the role you play as their educator.

23

VALUING EDUCATION

Most teachers will certainly *claim* to value education. As teachers, it is easy to claim a love for learning and espouse the value of education, but as with most proclaimed beliefs, actions often speak louder than words. What "valuing education" actually *looks* like in each classroom may depend on the teacher, the subject area, and the age of the students.

A simple example of what it looks like to value education can be illustrated with the longstanding joke in a small community school that "Mrs. D will never let her class watch a movie." While there is certainly a place and a purpose for viewing in curricula and films can provide rich learning opportunities, when the students say this about Mrs. D, it is more of a commentary on how other teachers use movies in their classrooms.

Too many students are accustomed to teachers using Friday afternoons, the day before a holiday, or the lack of a detailed sub-plan, as excuses to entertain and babysit the class with a movie rather than plan for an educational experience. When students good naturedly heckle Mrs. D about not getting to watch a movie in her class, it is actually a sign of the respect they have for her adherence to making class time worthwhile. The students understand that Mrs. D values her time with them too much to waste it with cheap entertainment with which students are already bombarded on a daily basis.

Valuing education means a conscientious, consistent, and deliberate refusal to waste time on distractions that cannot be tied to learning, be it academic or personal growth. That is not to say that teachers' conversations with students should never get sidetracked. There is a great deal of value in "wasting" time talking about the local team's hockey game the night before or chatting with students about their upcoming music concert. These kinds of moments and conversations are not time wasters, but rather relationship builders, and contribute to students' personal growth in a way that will also be reflected in their academic development.

When kids recognize that you see them as individual people with their own personalities, likes and dislikes, and do not lump them all together as mere beings in desks who are there for the next math lesson, they, in turn, do not see you as just a teacher. When they see you as an actual *person*, rather than just their teacher, then your passion for education becomes more real to them. This passion should permeate all that you do, and your students will witness it in your interactions with them, with their parents, and in the community.

WORKING HARD TO ACHIEVE AN EDUCATION

There should never be a single student who passes through your class who would not be able to say that you work hard at your job. It should simply be that obvious.

This does not, however, mean that teachers should brag about their work in order to win a badge of recognition or a "Hustler Award" like young kids receive at their amateur sporting events. Rather, there has to be a balance between boasting about the work you put into being a good teacher and making kids aware that good teaching requires significant effort.

The reason for working to achieve this balance is that when teachers make a secret of the work they put into preparing for their classes, they affirm students' belief that good teaching is simply a natural talent with which they happened to be blessed. Comments from students such as "Mr. T was born to be a teacher" insinuate a misled belief that quality teaching cannot be achieved unless, perhaps, the stars aligned when the teacher was born.

The concerning part of this perspective is that it then becomes easy for students to translate that belief into their understanding of academics and view the "smart" kids in class as being equally blessed the intelligence gene, rather than recognize those students' success as a result of hard work and dedication. Students need to be shown how to internalize success and learn from their failures so they cannot blame their lack of success on unfortunate phenomena that are out of their control. As with most lessons, this awareness of their ability to control the outcome of their academic endeavors with hard work and persistence is best learned when they see it happen first hand from their teachers.

When students see, understand, and recognize that they enjoy their favorite teacher's classes because the lessons they learn are the result of hours and hours of endless, sometimes boring, preparation and work, students can then apply that same understanding to their own work. If teachers do not model how to work hard and commit to pursuing excellence, then how can they possibly expect that from their students?

While it is not necessary to make an issue of advertising the time you spend on planning for the classroom routines that they have come to appreciate and expect, you do need to ensure that they are aware it does not just happen by magic.

For example, you might laughingly explain that the edges of their game pieces on the bulletin board are not exact because your youngest child was helping you cut them out late last night after his bedtime, as you were trying to get everything ready for the next day's lesson. Or maybe you will have to apologize to the student whose paper has a ketchup stain on it because you had it at the rink while you were trying to both mark essays and parent your kids by feeding your daughter fries while her brother was on the ice.

Whatever your stories might be, share some of those moments with your students so they can laugh with you and also come to appreciate the dedication you have to making their classroom experience enjoyable, memorable, and inspiring. It is not just what you say in your classroom that matters because the old adage that "actions speak louder than words" is a truth that students are very intuitive to pick up on. What you do is always going to be more important than what you say. This applies to every situation in the classroom, but explicitly so regarding students handing in assessments and the timeliness of your feedback and evaluation.

Effective teachers do not take more than two to three days (and preferably just one) to return assessments. This is an imperative golden rule for two reasons. The first reason is that students can only learn from their work if they receive timely feedback. A student once shared a story about her teacher who took six weeks to return her class's grade six science exam, an unfortunately all-too-common occurrence in every school. By the time the class finally received their exam results, the students could not even remember what the exam had been on, let alone reflect on what they had gotten wrong and have the opportunity to relearn the missed concepts.

You likely have similar stories and experiences where teachers you know procrastinate on getting their marking done until their students no longer even remember they wrote a particular assessment. Timely feedback is essential if students are going to learn from their mistakes.

The second reason is equally important, or perhaps even more important than the first. The other old saying that applies in this context is, of course, the title of the book. Teachers simply *must* "practice what you preach" when it comes to classroom expectations. Teachers should never give students assessment deadlines that they would not be willing to meet themselves.

There is little that is more frustrating to listen to in the staffroom than teachers who bemoan and complain about their students who never meet their deadlines or get their work done on time when, in other conversations, these same teachers admittedly joke about the mountain of marking they have let pile up on their desk over the last month that they will have to plow through before report card marks are due.

Why would students bother to hand anything in on time to teachers who cannot be bothered to mark and return it anyway?

If teachers want to *preach* to kids about the necessity of meeting deadlines in their classroom, they must also *practice* the effort that is required to provide tangible evidence of how hard work can yield results. When students exclaim over getting their exams back the next day, you might want to explain how you made that possible by sacrificing some of your own personal time. This helps students understand the relationship between hard work and results, and they will learn to respect you for it.

The best part of this lesson, however, is not only the respect they will give you for "walking the talk," but it comes back ten-fold on due dates (see previous chapter) because they are much more willing to do the work for you if they trust it will be reciprocated by you doing *your* work for *them*.

When teachers value education and work hard to make it a priority in their lives, kids tend to respond with similar values and work ethic. When you routinely share anecdotes like the ones above (ketchup on the assignment, jagged cutting) with your students, this reminds kids that you have a life beyond the classroom walls, a life that you do not put on hold because you are a teacher, but neither do you put your teaching on hold because you have a life.

When you find ways to meld the two together and show students how you find a balance between school and life, then they can learn to do the same. Encourage students to recognize the time they do have in their day, rather than allow them excuses of being "too busy" to complete their work. For example, do they have time between hockey and music lessons? Work through a couple of math questions. Waiting for dad at the office? Read a couple of chapters of your book.

In short, it comes down to teaching students to value the work they have been assigned and then make time in their day to work hard to complete it. They will soon enjoy the reward that awaits them when they are more prepared for exams and score better results on assignments that were not completed at the last minute.

GRIT IN THE FACE OF ADVERSITY

Educators face adversity in all shapes and sizes. In your career, you will likely teach students who challenge your authority, struggle within the confines of education systems that do not meet the needs of your kids, work with colleagues who do not share your vision, encounter parents who would rather blame the teacher than their own child for any perceived lack of success, and the list could go on. Teaching is not for the faint of heart and so it may come as a surprise to you that rather than dwell on the typical types of adversity an educator may face, this section of the chapter is going to focus instead on the well-intentioned philosophy of teacher advocacy organizations.

Way too often, organizations that advocate for educators' rights push agendas that seem to have teachers' best interests at heart but ultimately benefit the advocacy group and not the students. You may counter that it is exactly the point of these types of groups—to fight for the rights of the teacher and not those of the students—and you would not be wrong. There is a great deal of valuable work done by teachers' advocates that should not be discounted. It is unfortunate, however, when students' best interests are not always at the forefront of every educational decision that is made, even if it was possibly in the best interests of teachers. Humbling though it may be to acknowledge, teachers are not the ones for whom the education system was intended. The students are.

A teacher once commented that she had quit volunteering for extra-curricular activities in the school because the government did not respect teachers enough to grant them their contract demands. One might wonder in response to this mentality . . . who was this teacher volunteering for in the first place? Politicians or kids? And who is hurt by her stand against volunteering? Politicians or kids? Taking a stand on a political issue by refusing to coach or work with children likely did not hurt the politicians one iota. But it did hurt the kids.

Standing on the soapbox of teachers' rights may have given this teacher the excuse not to go the extra mile for her kids, but that is not a soapbox from which teachers should be preaching if they are concerned about what is best for kids.

Sometimes facing adversity means going against the tide of popular advocacy thought that protects teachers' rights to not volunteer their time beyond the required classroom hours and encourages teaches not to coach extra-curricular sports, organize clubs, or offer free academic support. While your rights not to volunteer extra time with students might be protected by your union or advocacy group, who is protecting the children's rights to quality education?

Quality education means more than delivering curriculum content between the 9:00–3:30 hours of instruction. Quality education means building relationships with students, offering them opportunities to learn and grow as people, developing their collaborative and teamwork skills, and teaching them about service to others. These aspects of quality education cannot be done justice if students are not given the extra-curricular opportunities that best foster those types of lessons.

Extra-curricular commitments allow you to share your own personal passions for sport, music, drama, debate, community leadership, environmental stewardship . . . whatever it may be, with your students. These activities allow you to get to know students on a personal level that cannot be replicated in the classroom. And they allow students to get to know you in a similar light, which teaches them to respect your commitment to them in a manner they will not have if your relationship remains contained within the four walls of a classroom.

When students witness you "practicing what you preach" regarding school involvement, they take those lessons forward and become the engaged employees and community members who understand the value of giving more than just the bare minimum because they have witnessed the rewards of giving more through your modeled example.

Many of the thoughts expressed in this chapter may horrify any teachers' union or advocacy group. After all, how can anyone be justified in challenging and encouraging teachers to give above and beyond the call of duty when "it is not part of their contract" and "they do not get paid for that"? Sadly, this "contract rights" perspective often culminates with the children becoming victims of a fight in which they have no say. When governments and unions disagree on teachers' rights, it is the students who become the collateral damage, caught between two groups who failed to put their needs first, and who do not receive the quality educational experience to which they are entitled.

The humbling reality is that most teachers make a good, comparable salary, especially when considering the holidays they are given in the year. A retired kindergarten teacher once shared her observation that the worst thing the government ever did was to pay teachers a salary that was competitive with other professions. The result of teachers' high salaries, she pointed out, was that now schools are filled with teachers who are there for the holidays, the pay, and the benefits, which means they are *not* there for the love of education, the sake of the school community, and—most importantly—the *kids*.

Obviously, that is a generalization as there are many teachers putting in countless, exhausting hours for the sake of their students who would have chosen to be educators regardless of the holidays, pay, and benefits, but if you critically consider some of your colleagues who never seem to be engaged with kids and constantly complain about their chosen profession, you might find that you agree with this observation.

Despite what it may sound like this chapter is encouraging, it is not actually necessary for you to take on so much that you break in order to be an effective teacher. Your mental and physical health are important, and you should not push yourself past the limits of what you can reasonably give. But on the other hand, it is absolutely true that the more you give to this profession, the more you will get out of it. If you want your students to push themselves to achieve their best, then as the educator responsible for setting those high expectations, you cannot, *CANNOT* expect less of yourself.

DENY THE "CHARMS OF COMPLACENCY"

When you have similarly high expectations of yourself, not only are you modelling the sense of responsibility and accountability you want your students to learn, but your investment in the kids for whom you are putting in that time becomes a joy instead of a chore. Angela Duckworth explores this same concept in her book *Grit*. She comments that she typically spends seventy-plus hours a week doing her job, sometimes at the expense of other things she would enjoy doing. But she has recognized that "when you really love what you do, you might find that you *want* to [work, and that] you do not want to take a vacation from your calling" (Duckworth 2016, 280).

When questioned if she regrets the sacrifices that this level of commitment to her work, and to being *gritty*, has required, Angela explained that her children are growing into young adults who have embraced their parents' "gritty" standards of excellence. Through witnessing their parents' commitment to the jobs that are their passion and the balance with time for their family life, Duckworth's children have "recognized that [while] complacency has its charms, none [are] worth trading for the fulfillment of realizing their potential" (Duckworth 2016, 271).

If you are not interested in, or willing to consider, embracing the demands of this career, perhaps this is not the profession for you. It is easy, probably far too easy, for teachers to become complacent in their jobs, particularly for those teachers who teach the same grades and the same subjects every year.

If you are in this type of repetitive position, challenge yourself to deny the "charms of complacency" and remember that despite the content being the same year after year, the unique individuals who are about to embark on the journey of learning that content are experiencing it for the first time. They bring with them all sorts of stories and backgrounds that have the potential to help make your experience with that same old content as unique as they are. After all, you are teaching *kids*, not *content*—kids who deserve your best, kids who will give you their best if you model that for them.

It may sound like you are being asked to sacrifice yourself until you drop dead from exhaustion, until you burn out of the passion with which you started your career, until you have nothing left to give your own family. The point of this chapter is to challenge you to push yourself, yes, but not to the extent where you can no longer be effective. Angela Watson, an educator who has dedicated her time to writing books and creating programs to help teachers manage their time, believes that "it is a myth that every teacher has to work endless unpaid hours to do a great job for kids. The truth is that working more hours does not equate with more effectiveness. It is what you do with the hours that makes a difference" (Watson 2019, 42).

You will have to find your own balance between working the hours Angela Duckworth embraces in order to be "gritty" and ensuring you are not over-extending yourself as Angela Watson cautions against. In finding that balance for yourself, you will experience the truth and the beauty of this profession—that "the more you give, the more you will receive."

Still unsure? Consider the message in this chapter from the point of view as a parent of your own children (if you do not have your own kids, please imagine for the sake of this exercise). What kind of teacher do you want for them? The kind who shows up at 9:00 and excuses themselves from the classroom at the end of the day, beating kids in the rush to the door? You may laugh, but you can likely identify the faces of your colleagues who do this.

Or do you want the kind of teacher who makes time in their day for your child, who is willing to work with your kid to find time for extra math help, whose concern for your child's progress has them searching that evening for additional learning resources that might help them understand the concept they missed in today's lesson, or who voluntarily comes early to practice to give your student athlete a few more minutes of focused practice time on the skill that needs polishing?

If you want the latter teacher for your own kids, then be that teacher for other people's children.

And when you have burned the candle at both ends and have nothing left to give, seek the healing gifts of space, peace, and silence (see chapter 5: "Let nature teach you"). Have tea with a friend, or maybe even with your students when they stay after class just to chat. Revel in the knowledge that your burned-out wick has lit the spark of so many other candles. And be assured that yours, too, will re-ignite after a period of rest. As teachers, we are blessed with that opportunity more than most professionals.

Chapter 4

Sharpen Each Other

"Iron sharpens iron, and one man sharpens another."

Proverbs 27:17

There is no limit to the number of studies that have been done that laud the benefits of competition. It spurs invention and innovation in business. It teaches athletes to reach higher and train harder. It encourages musicians to hone their skills and strive for perfection. In essence, competition produces the same results as when iron is used by blacksmiths to sharpen iron. Competition inspires motivation and causes "one man [to] sharpen another," resulting in both participants getting better, their abilities more refined, and their skills closer to excellence.

If this is true for businesspeople, athletes, and musicians, then the same must also be said for students. Indeed, proponents of competition advocate for it as an effective and necessary component in developing "important skills like resilience, perseverance, and tenacity" (Gordon 2020) in today's youth. Carol Dweck, author of *Mindset: The New Psychology of Success*, says she does not mind losing if she "can see improvement" (Dweck 2006).

Losing is not equivalent to failure when students are taught to embrace the lessons learned from the experience.

Unfortunately, however, many educational theorists have sworn off competition in schools because they perceive it to "lead children to envy winners, to dismiss losers" (Kohn 1992) and that rather than build character, competition sabotages self-esteem and ruins relationships. Kohn suggests collaboration in schools is a much better alternative to competition and teaches students to communicate with others, trust their peers, and accept those who are different from themselves.

Ironically, perhaps the debate regarding competition versus collaboration in education does not need to end with a winner. Despite the aversion most competition supporters have to an "everyone wins" philosophy, in this case, that might simply be the answer. Rather than having to choose to engage students in competition or collaboration, what if teachers provided opportunities to do both?

The Organisation for Economic Cooperation and Development (OECD) conducted research that supports both sides of the competition versus collaboration debate. The research viewed competition favorably, stating, "a competitive spirit may improve academic performance" (A. Echazarra 2020). The article goes on to also outline the benefits of collaboration, explaining that students in "co-operative environments were less afraid of failing" (A. Echazarra 2020).

Rather than view collaboration and competition as a dichotomy from which teachers must choose, consider regarding the optimal learning environment for students as a melding of the two approaches. Teachers who endeavor to build *collaborative competition* into their classroom routines reap the benefits of both approaches with engaged students who are challenged by the competitive environment and supported by the collaborative approach to learning.

RESEARCH INTO ACTION

A collaboratively competitive approach to teaching and learning not only sounds like an oxymoron but it likely leaves you wondering where to begin. What follows in this chapter are specific examples of daily routines where theme-based units have been established in which students work together to apply conceptual knowledge and collaborative skills to complete a culminating challenge. The results of this daily routine of theme-based units have not only helped students become better problem solvers and collaborators, but have also instilled in them an unprecedented appreciation and enthusiasm for learning.

It is important to note that although the ideas presented are taken from high school and elementary mathematics classrooms, the strategies for collaborative competition could easily be adapted to any area of study. Each example provides concrete applications of the key criteria in successfully establishing a competitively collaborative classroom environment that will both challenge and support your students:

1. determine a *relevant theme*;
2. use "game pieces" to *maintain engagement*;
3. create a *scoreboard* that prominently displays the theme;
4. plan a cumulative activity on "*game day*";
5. find ways to *involve every student*; and,

6. strategically vary the *team* composition when starting a new unit.

THEMATIC RELEVANCE

Probably the most important piece in developing a unit that inspires teamwork and learning is choosing a theme that will both engage students and showcase a real-world application of the concept they are studying. While finding a theme that meets these criteria might sound daunting, a quick Google search of applications of the concept you are working on can sometimes reveal enough ideas to jumpstart the imagination. Asking students for ideas, however, is equally as effective. They are a never-ending source of inspiration for creative ideas that, as hare-brained, far-fetched, and social media-inspired as they may initially seem, are sometimes the most brilliant and effective.

Examples

Clue: Inductive and Deductive Reasoning

Have you ever played the board game Clue? Or tried to escape from an escape room? These kinds of activities use the inductive and deductive reasoning that is taught in senior math classes. When students walk into class on the first day of the unit, they are greeted with a picture of their school's mascot on the board that depicts him laying on the floor with police tape around his body. Somewhat horrified, but definitely intrigued and engaged, students are then given a "WANTED" ad looking for detectives to help solve the murder mystery of their beloved mascot. They are told that throughout the course of the unit they must work as a team to earn the clues, and if they are successful, they will win a field trip to an escape room.

Following this "gruesome" introduction, students then play the board game *Clue* for the rest of the period, at the end of which they discuss the difference between making guesses to collect information (suspect, weapon, room) and making an accusation based on the evidence collected. After having laid the groundwork for understanding, students now have a context for learning the terminology of this field of mathematics; that the collection of evidence supports "inductive reasoning," making a guess is called a "conjecture" and proving their conjectures to be true is called "deductive reasoning."

Thus the stage is set for both the theme, a Clue-based murder mystery of their school mascot, and the mathematical unit, inductive and deductive reasoning.

Honeybees: Place value up to 1,000,000

While dressing up to introduce a new unit is not necessary, when the opportunity presents itself, consider embracing the chance to visually get your students excited and curious about what is coming next.

To set the stage for a unit on place value of large numbers, consider how much more engaging it would be for young students to see their teacher walk into class that day, dressed as a beekeeper. And rather than begin the lesson by routinely copying down a place value chart displayed on the board, what if students were shown a video clip of bees buzzing in a hive and asked how many bees they thought were on the screen? When these young students start enthusiastically answering "a million," "a zillion," "bazillions!," you know they are hooked and ready to start learning about the appropriate language of large numbers in a real-world context.

MAINTAIN ENGAGEMENT

For students to stay engaged in the chosen theme, and thus build the anticipation for the culminating activity, they need regular opportunities to collect and earn game pieces that will improve their chances for success at the end of the unit. These "game pieces" will look different in each theme as they will depend on the final activity that has been designed to cap off the unit. The opportunities to win game pieces can occur in a variety of ways, as described below, and portrayed in the examples that follow:

- *During instruction.* A question can be indicated as an opportunity to earn a game piece by covering it up with a picture that symbolizes the unit (e.g., magnifying glass for the Clue theme, honeybee for the beekeeper theme, gold coin for a treasure hunt theme). When the students recognize the opportunity is coming, they quickly hunker down with pencil and paper to solve the problem.
- *The challenge.* While it is motivating for students to earn game pieces on easy procedural questions that quickly engage them in the theme of the unit, it is even more rewarding for them to earn the pieces on conceptually difficult questions that may take them days to solve. In every unit, it is rewarding to pose at least one or two challenging questions that require a deeper level of thought and a more concentrated effort to solve, than the mere procedural game piece questions they are given during instruction.

While the game piece questions inspire motivation for learning, what is even more significant are the conceptual conversations that occur when students are working together to earn those pieces. In the examples that follow, you will notice students' thinking is exposed in a way that would not be as apparent without these opportunities for conversation. When students work together to answer the game piece questions, not only are students' misunderstandings often clarified by their teammate's explanation but listening to these discussions also provides the teacher an opportunity to determine which concepts may require further instruction.

While these conversations could occur with any type of group work, the reward of the game piece is a definite motivator for students to talk through the challenges and arrive at a response with which they are all satisfied. As teams converse, argue, debate, and come to a consensus in their determination to arrive at the answer that will result in the coveted game piece, the conceptual understanding that evolves because of those conversations, arguments, and debates is unprecedented.

Examples

Clue: Inductive and Deductive Reasoning (during instruction)

Unit themes and collaborative activities can be designed for a variety of student team configurations. This particular theme is developed for students to work as a class to earn the game pieces so they can work collaboratively on the final activity—solving their mascot's murder mystery.

When presented with a question that is indicated as a "clue" opportunity by the magnifying glass icon, students quickly work through the steps and arrive at their answer. When they are done, a student's name is drawn from an envelope and that student is given the opportunity to share their answer and earn the clue if they are correct. If they answer incorrectly, another name is drawn, and the opportunity passes to the next student.

When questions are answered correctly, the clues that provide evidence such as "A candlestick with the mascot's blood on it was found in Scarlett's yard" are eagerly read out loud and then posted on the "crime scene" evidence board displayed in the classroom.

As the evidence mounts and the clues continue to point students to the guilty character, it is highly entertaining to sit back and watch curriculum and life lessons become a reality. The conversations about the evidence are the best use of "inductive and deductive" reasoning a teacher could ever hope to achieve and are far more engaging than having them respond to stagnant questions in a textbook.

Honeybees: Place value up to 1,000,000 (challenging question)

In the honeybee unit where an elementary class is learning about place value of large numbers, students earn honeybee points in "Hive Teams" that are comprised of approximately four students. Although students may earn honeybee points through procedural-type questions during the instruction, the teacher may also pose a challenge question and announce that any team that solves the problem throughout the unit will receive bonus honeybee points.

The idea with challenge questions, as opposed to procedural, is that they require students to apply a deeper conceptual understanding of the concepts to solve the problem and should be revisited often throughout the unit. See below for an example of a challenge question in the elementary unit on place value:

Beekeeper's Challenge

Three beekeepers have counted the bees in their hives and have created a riddle for you to solve. Use the clues to determine how many bees the beekeepers may have counted in their hives.

- Greater than 4500
- Not a multiple of 5
- The nearest thousand is 8000
- If you round to the nearest ten, then you must round down

As students' understanding of place value grows, so too do their conversations around this challenge question. When it was first presented to the class, one team member commented that the number could not end in a five because of the second clue, while another student concluded that the first digit should be an eight. Both comments revealed some understanding of the information presented in the clues, but not complete comprehension of place value.

As students near the completion of their learning about place value, the teacher has them refer to the challenge question that was presented at the beginning of the unit. Their conversations now reveal some deeper-level thinking. Team Stinger's dialogue is captured below:

- "The clues 'greater than 4500' and 'nearest thousand is 8000' mean the digit in the thousands place could be either a 7 or an 8."
- "Yeah. If it's a 7, then the digit in the hundreds place will have to be a five or bigger so that it rounds up to 8000."
- "And if the thousands digit is an 8, then the hundreds place has to be a number from 0 to 4 to make sure it rounds down to 8000."

- "Okay, so we know that the digit in the thousands place is either a 7 or an 8 and we also have ideas for the hundreds place. What do we know about the number in the tens place?"

The conversations continue as students decipher the clues in terms of their understanding of place value. Once the Hive Teams are satisfied with their possible number of bees in the beekeepers' hives, they ask for confirmation from the teacher and, if they are correct, get to draw a honeybee game piece from the large manila envelope that has been appropriately named "The Main Hive." Each honeybee in the envelope is labeled with a place value from one to one hundred thousand, in either digits or words, and represents how many bees their team gets to add to their hive collection.

SCOREBOARD

What is a game or competition without a scoreboard? The best way to keep the competition alive throughout the unit, and for students to see the reward of their work, is a live representation of their progress. While not every unit necessarily has to have a specific scoreboard, this is an influential factor in the success of a theme as it is a compelling motivator when students can see how their team is doing in relation to others. Although some units are more challenging to design scoreboards for, the effort is worthwhile.

The key factor to designing an effective scoreboard is to determine how to visually contribute to the sense of competition and teamwork that continues to inspire engagement in the concepts. This scoreboard does not have to be typical in nature with a tally of points, it could be a "crime scene" strategy board during a unit on mathematical logic, a Disney *Car's* "Rational Racetrack" when teaching fractions, or a philosopher's point board in English language arts.

Regardless of the unit students are studying, the board should match the theme you have chosen to make it more engaging and the kids get excited about witnessing their progress. In some cases, these score boards become so interactive that other classes who are not participating in a particular activity will get engaged in watching the progress of the game and pick favorites to win, cheering on the students who are involved.

Depending on your school's configuration, you may be able to get another class involved in the game and the competition between your students and those in another teacher's class will quickly become a rivalry that not only makes for a fun unit, but also encourages some pretty intense learning.

It may seem like a lot of work to continually update the bulletin boards to reflect the theme's scoreboard, and it could certainly be overwhelming, but this is something many students are willing to give up a few minutes of their time before, after, or during school to help create. There are artists in every class who love the opportunity to put those skills on display.

Examples

Clue: Inductive and Deductive Reasoning

The "scoreboard" the students use for the murder mystery unit is not intended in the traditional sense of keeping score with a tally of points earned. Rather, the scoreboard in this unit is mimicked after a detective's office where the evidence is collected and patterns are explored. Each clue students earn throughout the course of the unit is recorded on the bulletin board, with suspects and weapons pinned to corresponding pieces of evidence and lines drawn to represent different correlations. It is messy, it is interactive, and it is entertaining to listen to the conversations that occur around this board!

Honeybees: Place value up to 1,000,000

The scoreboard for the honeybee and place value unit visually represents both the theme as well as the concept. Each Hive Team is given a "hive," on which they display the bees they collect throughout the course of the unit. The hive is simply a large piece of paper that is divided into place value columns where the bees will be placed according to the number printed on their wings.

GAME DAY

As with the chosen theme and engaging scoreboard, determining a culminating activity that is worth working towards is a key component in a successfully planned unit. The purpose of the learning, embedded within a relevant and engaging theme, intensifies throughout the unit when there is a "game day" awaiting the students at the conclusion of the unit. When kids know what they are working towards, then every piece they collect has more meaning and their desire to earn it is reflected in their motivation to work harder in class, complete their homework, and communicate with their team. It is a win-win situation all around.

Examples

Clue: Inductive and Deductive Reasoning

Over the course of the unit, students could have collected approximately thirty clues regarding their mascot's murder. Each clue contains different information that would lead to their ability to "deductively reason" the answers to "who, what, where, when, why, and how" regarding the mascot's untimely demise. When the unit ends and students have learned how to use inductive reasoning to make conjectures, eliminate unlikely theories based on counterexamples, filter through faulty proofs, and ultimately prove their conjectures using deductive reasoning, they then compile all their evidence and use those skills to solve the murder mystery.

Even the frustration they sometimes have with each other when trying to come to a decision regarding the five questions they are required to answer provides an opportunity for them to learn conflict resolution as well as how to persuade others with supporting evidence. Most classes correctly deduce the majority of the answers, but there are always one or two students who will groan in misery afterward when the correct responses are read that "I knew that was the answer, but no one would listen to me!" The victory prize on the line for this activity is a field trip to a local escape room where kids use their detective (i.e., inductive and deductive reasoning) skills to puzzle their way through the clues and make an escape.

Honeybees: Place value up to 1,000,000

By the end of the place value unit, the hives will be filled with the honeybee game pieces that the Hive Teams have collected. Students become "beekeepers" on the final day of the unit and are given a clipboard of questions pertaining to the hives displayed in the classroom. In their Hive Teams, students will work together to answer questions such as:

- Which hive has the most bees? How do you know?
- Team Stinger's hive has 12 bees in the thousands spot. Explain how many bees that represents.
- How many more bees does Team Queen have than Team Buzz?
- Write out Team Yellow's total number of bees in words and in expanded notation.

If possible, culminating the beekeeper's review activity with a visit from an actual beekeeper, either in person or virtually, would not only provide a fascinating learning experience for the students but may also hit the additional goal of finding a cross-curricular connection with outcomes in science. And, of course, a snack with biscuits and honey would be a pretty "sweet" way to finish the learning!

INVOLVE EVERY STUDENT

It is imperative to continually change how students earn game pieces to ensure all students stay engaged. A proponent of competition and collaboration in classrooms, Echazarra (2020) cautions that for "teamwork to function successfully, researchers have recommended meeting some conditions, such as ensuring that students acquire leadership and communication skills, making the goals of team members interdependent and establishing some kind of individual accountability." Here are a few ways teachers can ensure interdependence and individual accountability during the competition questions to earn a game piece:

- *Each group is given a different question.* Rather than have each group answer the same question, groups can be given a problem that is uniquely their own. After the teams have had a chance to complete their given question, they can work through it on the board. If the entire class is satisfied that their work is complete and accurate, that group earns the game piece. It adds an element of fun to allow another team to challenge the presenting team's answers if they see a mistake and "steal" that team's game piece.
- *Choose the group that answers.* In this scenario, every team is given the same question and once they have all had time to complete it, a team's name is randomly drawn from an envelope and that team gets the opportunity to answer it correctly and therefore earn the game piece. If they are incorrect, another team's name is drawn, and they get the opportunity that was missed by the previous team's wrong attempt.
- *Teacher chooses who explains.* To avoid the situation where teams with students who tend to work more quickly earn all of the game pieces, assign each student on the team a number or a role and randomly select a group member to respond to the question. If team member #3, for example, cannot explain their team's answer, then the second team that finished gets to respond in hopes of earning the game piece. This method puts pressure on each team member to understand the question and it encourages the student who finishes the question very quickly to slow down and explain their thinking to their team members rather than rush through the question on their own.
- *Assignment completion.* Reward any team whose group members have all completed their assigned practice questions from the day before with

a game piece. This is an effective way to motivate a class if they seem to be falling behind or failing to get their work done, and if necessary, might need to be the ONLY way students can earn a game piece if they need to be challenged to stay on top of their assignments.

MAKING TEAMS

Once your planning is complete and you have the idea for the game established, a system for collecting points, a scoreboard to track those points, and an ultimate challenge to work toward as a culminating activity, then it is time to divide the class into teams . . . and you should always choose the teams. This is not the time for kids to stack their team, pick their friends, or neglect the poor student who always gets left out. If you are teaching leadership and teamwork in the midst of adding and subtracting fractions, for example, then it is necessary to avoid the underlying popularity contest that is inevitable when kids pick their own teams.

Depending on the theme of the unit and the strategy of the game, students can be divided in various ways, and the more you vary the group configurations for different units, the more they will anticipate their new group when the unit changes. It is critical that the creation of the teams results in a level playing field so as not to create frustration and hopelessness in a team that gets left in the dust. Regularly changing the structure of the teams enhances the level of competitiveness by giving students different team dynamics.

It is fun for them to work together as one large team against the teacher to collect game pieces, other times they could be split into two teams with their desks physically arranged to face each other in a debate-style structure, or they could be divided into what is probably the most common configuration with pods of three or more kids. Once the students have their teams and have collaborated in the first moments of the unit by giving themselves a team name, thereby establishing themselves an identity, then the games begin.

The variation in structure keeps students interested because when they arrive to class and the desks are arranged differently on the first day of a new unit, they are immediately intrigued to see what is coming next. This typically involves a lot of desk shuffling because the game structure in second period, for example, may not be the same as in period three, but kids tend to sort that kind of thing out relatively quickly once a routine is established and the two minutes it takes them to move desks into their class's arrangement is worth their engagement the rest of the period.

COLLABORATIVE COMPETITION: WORTH THE EFFORT

The type of competitive collaboration described in the previous examples of theme-based units does not happen overnight. These types of units require planning, preparation, and a commitment to providing a learning experience for students that goes beyond the routine. But when you overhear comments such as "this is why I LOVE this math class!" from a student who is peering through the "crime-scene" cordoned-off library door to the "murdered" school mascot . . . the effort becomes worth it. Who does not want to hear that kind of validation as a teacher?

The rewards you will experience for revising your delivery of curriculum content to include theme-based lessons that inspire competitive collaboration and give students a purpose for their learning will be immediate and tangible. Students will pile eagerly into your classroom when the bell rings to check the "scoreboard" for the unit to see their daily progress; the classroom soundtrack will be a satisfying mixture of laughter and intense focus as they work together to compete for game pieces; and students' conversations will reveal a deeper conceptual understanding of the concepts they are learning.

Perhaps most rewarding of all, you will witness students' appreciation for their peers when they work, not just as classmates, but as teammates, who are striving for the same goal. In short, the combination of creating a collaboratively competitive classroom will have your students "sharpening each other"; both in regard to academic skills, but even more importantly, in regard to interpersonal skills.

Chapter 5

Let Nature Teach You

> *"But ask the beasts, and they will teach you; the birds of the heavens, and they will tell you; or the bushes of the earth, and they will teach you; and the fish of the sea will declare to you."*
>
> Job 12:7

Teachers can creatively turn their classrooms into engaging learning environments where students can be challenged to solve authentic problems. But regardless of how creative a teacher might be in offering contextual learning opportunities to students, the four walls of an indoor classroom simply minimize the potential for learning that can be explored when the sky is, quite literally, the limit.

Place-based education, experiential learning, outdoor school, environmental education . . . regardless of the current catchphrase used to describe the type of education where teachers take their students beyond the four classroom walls, they all offer students the opportunity to learn from, and within, the most elemental and fundamental classroom that exists: nature.

The benefits of natural learning have been studied for decades and the number of hits on a quick internet search reveal the staggering evidence that supports this type of education. Everything from magazine articles, scholarly journal entries, and teachers' blogs have been written to capture the ways in which students benefit from learning outdoors.

If you spend even a few minutes scanning websites that are devoted to outdoor education, you will read things like it "builds community and culture, raises expectations and standards, increases connection between students" (Becker, 2016) or it "improves students' engagement in and motivation for learning" (Williams, 2017). Research has even been done to prove the value in outdoor experiential learning for both gifted and special needs students.

With the research done to support outdoor learning environments, it would seem imperative, then, that teachers find ways to get students out of the building and that schools find ways to support these initiatives.

How this is done will, and should, look different in every situation as clearly what works best for a grade two class will not be as effective in a senior literature course. But do not let your grade level or subject area be an excuse for you to disregard the ways nature could enhance your students' learning experience. Although there is no prescriptive formula that can guarantee a successful immersion of your students in the great outdoors, there are a plethora of tried and true examples available from which you can build your own adventures.

There are varying degrees of how the natural world can be infused into students' learning, or how students' learning can be infused into the natural world. Some school districts have created survivalist- type programs where core subjects like math and reading are taught alongside wilderness first aid and shelter-building on multiple day excursions throughout an entire term. Other teachers who are more bound by classroom limitations have found ways to connect their instruction to the environments that surround them with day trips or shorter forays into the outdoors.

Both the survivalist and day-trip type of learning experiences will be explored in detail in this chapter, but note that regardless of the number of minutes, hours, or days you expose your students to authentic learning outside the classroom walls, they will reap the benefits of each exposure.

SURVIVALIST LEARNING: OUTDOOR SCHOOL

Imagine a classroom where teaching quadratic functions is demonstrated by making the sweeping arc of a parabola in the water with a paddle as students canoe the mighty Churchill River.

Imagine a classroom where studying poetry means reading Rudyard Kipling's poem "If" by firelight, discussing what it means "to be a man, my son" and how one can aspire to such greatness.

Imagine a classroom experiencing firsthand how glaciers were responsible for landscape formations when hiking along a trail and pausing to learn the origins of a seemingly misplaced erratic.

Imagine a classroom where students learn the necessity of being "proud to poop" because holding it in for a ten-day camping trip to wait for a toilet is simply not healthy.

Survivalist types of outdoor school programs provide these kinds of experiences, and more. Depending on the school and goal of the program, however, the delivery of these experiences will look different. Some of these programs are immersive and last for a full term, either beginning in September and lasting until January or starting in January and ending in June. Other programs may be excursion-based and offer students one or two trips throughout the year rather than expecting a full-term commitment from staff and students.

Typically, the middle school or high school students who choose to enroll in immersive types of experiential learning programs study the regular subjects that their in-school counterparts are learning; they simply do so without the constraints of four walls around them. Rather than sit in a desk and watch the slides go by on a Smartboard screen, these students will sit around a campfire, or in a bus seat as they travel, and learn from the teacher's lessons on a portable whiteboard.

When these outdoor students are not "in class" around the campfire or on a bus, they are hiking, cycling, or paddling their way through various adventures that provide them with memorable learning opportunities that are impossible to achieve any other way. Most of these types of semester-long programs begin with short excursions that last for one or two nights until students get comfortable with the routines of living in the wilderness. As students gain the required skills, the journeys lengthen until they are able to spend many consecutive days away from civilization. They return from these excursions to spend a few days at home visiting family, cleaning and maintaining their gear, and preparing for their next adventure.

Teaching a survivalist outdoor experiential program is certainly about helping students develop a skill set and exposing them to a particular lifestyle, but above all, it teaches kids about teamwork in a way that can never be replicated in any regular classroom setting.

When students are essentially living out in the bush with the same group of people for months on end with only a few days at home between trips, they are forced to learn very quickly to put aside differences and work through challenges together. That is not to say there will not be disagreements that may even escalate to heated arguments and fights over everything from how to set up a tent to who has the best paddling j-stroke. Personalities will clash and without doors to slam, rooms to which they can escape, or technology to provide a distraction, conflicts are unavoidable.

Amid those battles, however, are valuable life lessons about dealing with conflict and coming out on the other side better for having seen both sides of the issue.

In addition to conflict-resolution and survival skills, students who enroll in nature-based programs develop an unprecedented appreciation for, and desire to protect, the natural world in which they are immersed. Teaching about "no trace camping" and sustainability is far more effective when it is part of the daily routine rather than a concept in a textbook.

When students come across a campsite whose previous users were not respectful of the commonly accepted camping etiquette, they witness the effects of that disrespect and the devastation it can have on the wilderness. Seeing garbage lying around and birch trees stripped of their bark in a selfish desire to have good fire-starting material, students in these programs understand on a different level how important it is to care for the natural resources that are so fragile and vulnerable. It becomes apparent very quickly in these situations how much of an impact each person's ecological footprint can have if one does not tread with care.

There is so much to be learned from nature itself, and from those whose experience in nature can teach you how to become a part of it, rather than just a user of it. Although these reflections thus far have focused on survivalist type nature educational programs, they are understandably not practical for every school, teacher, or student. There are, however, components of such survivalist school experiences that can be adapted for use in other courses, for other students, and by any teacher.

SOLO TIME

One of the challenges that students in a northern Saskatchewan "Outdoor School" experience learn to embrace is wilderness solo time. These kids gradually develop a tenacious sense of endurance throughout the term, both in their ability to withstand the elements as outdoor conditions and temperatures steadily decrease throughout the fall, as well as in their ability to be comfortable with their own company as their mere minutes of solo time steadily increase to hours throughout the term.

Regardless of the amount of time they have to spend in solitude, there is an unbending rule that these students cannot use technology nor talk to anyone in that time. As their survival skills develop, so too does their length of solo time grow. They begin the term by being sent out on their own for ten minutes, then an hour, then several hours, with nothing but a journal in which they can reflect on their experience or plant assignments that are designed to help them focus on the flora that surrounds them.

The solo time exercises culminate when they proudly accomplish the feat of "surviving" on their own, in a shelter they have built, for twenty-four hours. In the Saskatchewan wilderness conditions of November, that accomplishment is no small triumph. Not many people would have the tenacity or the skills to do what these young adults do, nor have their strength of character and determined sense of perseverance.

Spending twenty-four hours alone in the wilderness is not necessarily realistic for everyone, nor is it practical for every teacher to build such a phenomenon into their classroom routine. This type of activity is intended for specialized programs whose focus is wilderness survival in addition to academic learning. What is realistic, however, and maybe even necessary in every classroom, are the benefits of providing students with outdoor solo time, no matter how long.

Consider making time in your lesson plans to regularly provide students the opportunity to physically distance themselves from each other outside. They may choose a spot by water, some may climb a tree, and others might be content to simply lay down on a grassy open space. Their chosen spot is irrelevant, but what *is* important is that kids are given at least ten minutes of solo time at least once a week to think about whatever needs their attention the most in that moment. You may want to provide them with a couple of quotes as reflection prompts if they are stuck, but the key to solo time is not to *assign* work; this is not a time for reading and working. It is a time for just *being*.

Most students are accustomed to the type of solo time whose silence is dispelled by the chatter from a T.V., the ping of a cell phone, or the raucous entertainment on another electronic device. Some might be accustomed to the type of silence whose space is filled with books and their thoughts consumed with a plot. For most students, however, ten minutes of forced solo time without some avenue of entertainment to distract them is a novelty. Many people, students and adults alike, are not used to being entirely alone with their thoughts and are not always comfortable with no tools to distract them from themselves.

It is this discomfort that helps students begin to reflect inward and ultimately helps them become more certain and confident in themselves. If you can create a space where students become so familiar with this routine of quiet solitude, and so respectful of each other that they are comfortable sharing how they spent that solo time, you will be amazed at where their minds and thoughts have taken them in those moments. Not only will these opportunities help you to truly know your students, but over time they come to truly know themselves.

One of the beautiful rewards of regularly implementing solo time is that by the time students settle into the moment and begin to appreciate the sense of quiet, their time is usually up, and the experience leaves them wanting more . . . which, as teachers all know, is exactly how you want to end a lesson.

PRACTICING WHAT YOU PREACH: NATURAL LESSONS

Solo time is a simple and easy way to begin incorporating nature into classroom routines that does not take much planning or time. There are, however, a plethora of other ways this valuable lesson of allowing nature to be the teacher can be embedded in other curriculum content that does not require days' worth of dedicated trips and excursions.

Science teachers should have almost no trouble finding ways to engage students in outdoor learning. Volunteer your class to help with the community garden plot or build your own set of garden boxes in the school grounds for students to use to study plant biology and growth. Plan a hike to a nearby river or pond to explore the native aquatic life, of which many students are completely unaware exists. Seek opportunities to visit local organizations or businesses that are intrinsically connected to the land and learn from them the importance of environmental sustainability.

For those educators who are responsible for teaching about society and humanity, consider taking your children on an urban trek. Have them research the history of the buildings in the place they call home and present what they learned to the class as they walk around their community. There are so many opportunities to not only take your students outside with the content in social science curricula, but also to engage them in the community, which will only enrich their learning.

Teachers of literature might consider reading a poem or an essay with their students as they pause on a hike in a nearby park. If possible, extend the hike to include building a fire, having lunch, and enjoying the companionship that can only be found in remote spaces where the sole entertainment is each other and the beauty of nature. As students immerse themselves in their surroundings, provide them with opportunities to use the scenery as a writing prompt.

Math teachers might find ways to incorporate the concepts of graphing by superimposing a Cartesian plane on a map of the community and having students graph equations that lead them to the next clue on a graphing treasure hunt. Or perhaps students might measure plant growth or tabulate species varieties and then calculate statistical data on the information they collect.

Regardless of the subject area, nature is conducive to lessons that cannot be taught indoors. You may disagree and feel daunted by the impossible task of forcing nature into a curriculum where it seemingly has no place. Do not give up before you give it a chance! And if in doubt, use a classic student strategy and begin by searching online for answers. Although technology should be pocketed when on outdoor learning excursions for the sake of focusing on the surroundings, use it to your advantage in planning these activities by searching for, and borrowing, ideas from teachers who have already trod this path of natural learning.

Teachers around the globe have found ways to weave curriculum content into the natural world and have willingly shared it in blogs and websites. As an education university professor once jokingly quipped, "the best teachers are those who beg, borrow, and steal from their colleagues." In the global village in which we now live, it is so easy to beg, borrow, and steal from amazing educators who share your passion for your subject area. When teachers are willing to share their work, and willing to humble themselves to recognize they are better when they borrow from each other's experiences, the ones who benefit are the ones who most deserve this effort: the students.

THE WILDERNESS IDEA

One piece of literature that may help convince you of the importance of infusing natural learning into your curriculum, and that you may consider assigning to higher level readers, is a letter written by Wallace Stegner to the Outdoor Recreation Resources Review Commission in California. In his letter, Stegner asks the Commission to preserve some of the remaining wilderness, not for the sake of recreation, but for sanity of all people. In his letter, he passionately and metaphorically argues that mankind's technological "progress" has not only "brought us increased comfort and more material goods, it has [also] brought us spiritual losses, and it threatens now to become the Frankenstein that will destroy us."

Stegner's letter was written in 1960. Stegner was concerned about the advancements of modern society taking over humanity. If he were to write this same letter now, more than half a century later, what would he think of the technological progress that he perceived to be a threat back in 1960?

Stegner's premise is similar to the belief that although excursions in the wilderness are valuable for teaching life lessons, survival skills, teamwork, and respect for nature, you do not actually need to live these experiences to benefit from what the wilderness has to offer. It is the affirmation, the absolute certainty, that this wilderness exists, that allows the human race to slow their minds in the midst of the demanding chaos that daily confounds them and breathe deeply with the reminder that they are . . . okay.

Providing students the opportunities to experience this wilderness space offers a reassuring certainty that there is "something" out there that is bigger than the conflicts they might face and larger than the battles in which they engage, regardless of the turmoil in their lives. That "something" is dubbed by Stegner as the "wilderness idea." His eloquent definition deserves space in this chapter.

> Something will have gone out of us as a people if we ever let the remaining wilderness be destroyed; if we permit the last virgin forests to be turned into comic books and plastic cigarette cases; if we drive the few remaining members of the wild species into zoos or to extinction; if we pollute the last clear air and dirty the last clean streams and push our paved roads through the last of the

silence, so that never again will Americans be free in their own country from the noise, the exhausts, the stinks of human and automotive waste. And so that never again can we have the chance to see ourselves single, separate, vertical and individual in the world, part of the environment of trees and rocks and soil, brother to the other animals, part of the natural world and competent to belong in it. . . . We need wilderness preserved—as much of it as is still left, and as many kinds—because it was the challenge against which our character as a people was formed. The reminder and the reassurance that it is still there is good for our spiritual health even if we never once in ten years set foot in it. It is good for us when we are young, because of the incomparable sanity it can bring briefly, as vacation and rest, into our insane lives. It is important to us when we are old simply because it is there—important, that is, simply as an idea (Stegner, 1960).

Think about some of the students you know who are hurting, struggling, and floundering. Then consider the peace and the gentle but soul-deep reminder that being outdoors in silence can afford. These hurting and struggling kids need to experience those moments of knowing that, although *everything* may not be okay, for a moment, *they* can be. Everyone needs such a space, a place where just being in it gives you a sense of the world's grandeur that helps you put life in perspective. Parents, educators, and adults who work with children all have an obligation to teach kids about the importance of such a space where solo time and nature's peace can subdue raw emotions and calm troubled thoughts.

If kids are not taught the importance of *space*, of *solitude*, of *knowing* in a way that is deeper and more profound than any other knowledge they will gain, that they are an incredible and valuable piece in a world so large that the fact they exist in it is miraculous, how can they ever be expected to see their own value? Where else, and how else, can they learn the "geography of hope" that Stegner insists will "reassure our sanity as creatures" is out there waiting for them, unless they are taught to seek it?

Chapter 6

Turning Suffering to Hope

"Suffering produces endurance, and endurance produces character, and character produces hope."

Romans 5:4

There is an indisputable joy that can be derived from teaching—a beauty of working with kids, a reverent feeling of reward that comes from witnessing learning as it happens, and a sense of blessedness in being part of the lives of these incredible people who will go out into the world and make it a better place.

But that is not to say teaching never hurts.

The unfortunate reality is that, as you well know, life is not all unicorns and rainbows. Life is messy and at times very painful. The children who walk into your classroom often have stories that have the power to destroy any adult who tried to walk a day in their shoes. Stories like the following . . .

- A student sought ways to avoid the pain he was feeling inside by causing pain he could experience on the outside. Scared, confused, and hurting, he would text his only trusted confidante, his English teacher, at 2:00 a.m. with the words, *I am cutting.*
- A grade nine student, a mere 14-year-old child, hesitantly confided in her teacher that she was pregnant and asked for help to tell her parents because she was afraid of their response.
- A student in a senior English class wrote a letter to her childhood sexual abuser for a writing assignment that was innocuously intended for students to use as an authentic opportunity to address a concern they had regarding a social issue. While some students wrote to politicians and others to video game producers, she chose to write to the man who had left her crying on the cold bathroom floor.

- When he was 13, a grade eight student lost his grandfather. While this may hardly seem like a devastation worth including in this list, the rest of his story begs compassion. This young teenager had never met his father and his mom was in jail. The only constant source of love and stability this child knew was his grandfather, and now even he was gone from his life.
- Two brothers were in the back seat when the car their dad was driving ran into a harvester on the road. The header of the combine effectively ripped the hood off their car, and the life out of their parents.
- A month before graduation, a mentally delayed student who had obsessed over a beautiful and popular classmate since they attended kindergarten together, stabbed her multiple times with a steak knife in the hallway between classes.
- The daughter of a church pastor not only lived through the relatively common trauma of her parents getting divorced when she was in grade 11, but she also experienced the embarrassment, horror, and devastation of having her mom leave her dad because he had been accused of sexually assaulting a young member of their congregation. The core of all she knew—family and faith—was torn apart.

These are just a few true stories of student anguish, and you could likely add some that are equally as painful. While these stories are traumatic and devastating, they are not the only stories that hurt. Kids receiving text messages that they are "fat and ugly," having pictures taken of them over the bathroom stall while they are going to the washroom and then shared to social media, being shunned from a group of friends . . . the daily life of being a kid is painful enough without even considering the other stories that would essentially make it unbearable.

Yet somehow kids' resilience keeps them coming back to school, back to the classroom, and back to their teacher, despite the turbulence at home and in their personal lives. These children have an ability to endure and a strength to persevere that is both humbling and inspiring.

While some of these suffering children endure and persevere with quiet fortitude, others react in ways that make them challenging to love and support. But even when their behavior is difficult to embrace, it is imperative that their teachers find ways to see through that external reaction to the messy story that is their lives and love them anyway. These kids deserve a place that does not hurt them and they deserve to be welcomed by someone who is safe. It is a teacher's job to offer themselves and their classroom as that sanctuary.

It could be, and has been, argued that teachers should not be responsible for this type of work; that educators are trained to teach, they are not psychologists qualified to heal and that they therefore cannot be held accountable for dealing with the trauma of students' lives. While this may be true, and you may feel woefully inadequate when it comes to knowing how to respond to kids' pain, keep in mind that you are a constant presence for these kids, quite possibly the only stable influence with the potential to keep them afloat in the riptides of their lives.

Your constant presence is more than these kids often receive at home. This truth obligates teachers to not only *be* a constant and buoyant presence, but to be so with kindness, compassion, and tolerance in a way that escapes these children in other facets of their lives.

The other unfortunate reality, besides the truth that life is not all unicorns and rainbows, is that when kids are hurting, they will often deliberately hurt you. They will lash out in their own frustration and anger and blame you for the circumstances that they long to control, but either cannot or simply have not figured out how to yet. These same people who daily gift you with the joy of their presence may also at times make you wonder, momentarily, if it is worth it.

It is *always* worth it.

There is never a child who is not worth your time, your effort, your consideration, and your respect. Never. Even when they are hurting themselves or when they are intentionally trying to hurt you.

A grade six student who, after being caught swearing in class and, as per the school policy at the time, was required to be taken directly to the office, lashed out with venom and hatred. In his anger and frustration, he turned to his teacher as she walked with him down the hallway and told her that the only reason he could not learn was because she was the worst teacher ever and that she did not know how to teach. Recognizing his outburst for what it was, the teacher calmly replied, "I know it sucks to be in trouble. It is easy to blame others when we feel that way." And she left it at that.

After all, what would have been the point in further engaging this angry student in an argument and forcing an apology that he would not have sincerely felt at that moment? The teacher put the incident aside in her mind; the student served his consequence for swearing, and he returned to her classroom the next day with a bit of a chip on his shoulder for having been caught—both at swearing and at having thrown a tantrum in the hallway afterward.

Although the relationship between this teacher and student did not immediately improve, over the next couple of years, they became closer; they constantly nattered at each other over whether the Flames or the Oilers were the best NHL team, they became good-natured rivals during school spirit activities, and they developed a mutual respect for, and enjoyment of, each other.

Every teacher has similar stories of feeling sucker-punched to the gut by the kids for whom you sacrifice so much, only to be left feeling unappreciated and undervalued. The key to working with kids is understanding that their emotions and outbursts are 99% of the time a symptom of something else going on inside of them.

There are multitudes of wonderful books written on the topic of child psychology that provide various reasons for children's impulsive behavior, but as Dr. Jody Carrington explains, "kids are not attention-seeking, they are connection-seeking" (2019). It is truly that simple. Kids may go about it in the worst possible way, but their hurtful behavior is often an indication that they are lacking a connection to a trustworthy adult who loves and supports them unconditionally.

The hurt that these precious humans in your classroom cause cannot for a second overshadow the joy they can also give. As their teacher, the mature adult who *can* control your reaction to their behavior . . . you get to choose on which of those you dwell. The hurt or the joy. Is it even a choice?

When you consistently choose to seek and focus on the joy that *can* be found in each and every child you work with, the kids notice. No, they are not going to be able to explicitly define what you are doing and say, "That Mr. Smith. He is always looking for the best in me. He finds joy in working with me even when I am giving him a hard time." Kids are not quite that astute nor are they quite that garrulous. But they will show in other ways that they understand and appreciate your attitude.

This gratitude will be apparent when they hang out in your classroom at lunch if you happen to be there trying to catch up on marking. It will be apparent when they linger after last class, even on a Friday afternoon, to chat about everything and anything, before taking off to start their weekend. It will be apparent when they bring you gifts that reflect how they see you (a mug that says "Best Teacher"—and they mean it, an anime caricature of you with a quote bubble that captures your favorite classroom slogan, your go-to brand of tea or coffee).

The most significant way this gratitude will be apparent is when they come to you with their problems, their tears, and their hurts because they trust you, if not to fix them, then to listen with patience, understanding, and without judgment.

That unconditional acceptance and refusal to judge is the one small and tiny way that you can begin to heal the multiple wounds and lacerations of the souls in your classroom. Simply demonstrating to them that they are worthy of your time and your respect can provide them a sense of hope to persevere because someone has shown them they are worth it.

This demonstration of their worthiness must be more than a philosophy; as with the other values "preached" in this book, the demonstration of their worthiness must be a practice that is put into action. If these children are going to learn how to *endure* their *suffering* so that they can develop a strength of *character* that will allow them to *hope* for a better future, teachers cannot merely tell kids that "I'm here for you." Kids must see that this is true in order to trust that promise can be relied upon when they need it the most. It is in those relationships, when hurting students know they have someone in their corner, that they have a chance to turn their suffering into hope.

TEA TIME: SHOWING THEM THEY ARE WORTH IT

Although there are many ways teachers can convey to students that they are valued, honored and worthy of the teacher's time, one simple and subtle action a teacher can take is to offer "tea-time."

You know the cupboard in any school's staffroom that contains a random assortment of chipped, stained, and mismatched mugs that have been collected through generations of school staff who have come, gone, and left their mark by leaving behind their well-used mug? Consider having a similar collection in your classroom, displayed on one of those electrical trolleys teachers used to wheel around with a T.V. or projector on top, before the days of smartboards and other technology that revolutionized education.

Perched on top of that trolley with the collection of mugs, you will want to add a tea kettle (that may or may not be a fire-code violation), a jar of honey (some kids will need the natural sweetener) and an assortment of tea boxes, bags, and canisters that would rival any grocery store's tea aisle (do not worry—the students will enthusiastically add to your collection over time).

In addition to the physical presence of the tea cart in your room, ensure students are aware of your desire to have them make use of it. If you teach English, for example, you may want to put a note in your course syllabus that explicitly invites students to take advantage of your love for both tea and books by engaging with you in a conversation about literature while sipping your favorite hot beverage. If you teach math, perhaps your 7:30 morning math help sessions always begin with the kettle boiled and ready, waiting for the kids to trickle in with sleep in their eyes as they help themselves to tea before settling in to go over some questions.

This "tea cart" in your classroom, when used regularly and with deliberation, will come to symbolize for your students your standing invitation to chat over a cup of tea. More importantly, it will symbolize the fact that you see them as worthy of your time beyond the hours you are getting paid to teach them. Something as simple as inviting kids to share a cup of tea and conversation is putting the "I'm here for you" phrase into action in a way that is not intrusive, overwhelming, or daunting for students. Kids will come to sense that your willingness to meet them at the table means that you are also willing to listen to whatever else is on their minds. These conversations sometimes become real and they can become very raw.

The other thing you will likely notice as the tea habit evolves in your classroom is that this simple strategy becomes something more than just tea and conversations: it becomes an overall classroom atmosphere. Students' writing will become more personally eloquent, their Quick Writes (more on those in chapter 8) more honestly revealing, and their respect for each other more evident in their words and actions.

This habit of offering tea and conversation will turn the academic atmosphere of the classroom into a place where students can relax and be themselves; a place where they can see you as part of the community of learning with them, rather than just the dispenser of knowledge. And although you may begin these habits with this goal in mind, kids have a way of taking good ideas, making them their own, and often making them better. Over the years, it is likely that your collections of mugs and tea will grow to represent kids' favorite tea choices, flavored honey that "you just have to try," Donald Duck mugs, and likely even hot chocolate and marshmallows.

Certainly, it is not the actual tea (or hot chocolate) itself that will support these hurting kids through tough times in their lives. It is what the tea stands for—an adult in their life who is willing to share their time, engage in real conversation, and genuinely care. Sipping tea with kids cannot possibly solve some of the heartbreaking problems described at the beginning of this chapter, but these children, whose sorrows and woes far exceed most of ours, are better served and stand a better chance at finding a way out of the mess that has become their lives, if they are taught in an environment where someone cares enough to take the time to have tea with them.

Teaching hurts. But it only hurts if you are completely invested in the profession, not because you enjoy the 8:30–3:30 hours and holidays that teaching can afford. And if you are completely invested in this profession, you will not only have suffered alongside your hurting children, you will also have experienced the joy of working with kids and recognize there is more joy waiting for you if you pursue it. The old adage is true that the more you give, the more you will receive. Nowhere else in life will you find that to be more true than in working with kids, whether it is in a classroom, on a ball diamond, in the gym, on the track, or paddling down a river.

If you do not care that much, you will not hurt that much either. But then, neither will you find the joy that this profession has to offer . . . and how heartbreaking if you are a teacher and never find these blessings which make this career the most rewarding of all. The beauty of making time for tea with your students, or however you choose to show your kids that they are worth your time, is that it becomes easier with every cup to see them as the beautiful creations they are. Their hurtful stories that prompt them to act in ways that are anything but beautiful become secondary to the souls that lie beneath the story.

Take the time and find ways to seek joy in these kids because it is there, waiting for you. And you will find it if you look for it. Every time. What is more, you will reap that joy ten-fold . . . a thousand-fold . . . in return.

Chapter 7

Teach You Again

> *"For though by this time you ought to be teachers, you need someone to teach you again the basic principles."*
>
> Hebrews 5:12

Every educator, upon completion of their post-secondary education, receives a piece of paper that confirms their ability to do what many people would be afraid to even attempt. This paper document not only confirms that the owner is capable of surviving in a classroom filled with children, but also that they now have the ability to inspire, nurture, and educate these children. That piece of paper, otherwise known as an "education degree," implies that, once bestowed upon successful graduates, the receiver is now prepared to go out in the world . . . and teach.

The truth is, no amount of post-secondary education or professional development can possibly prepare teachers for every scenario they will encounter in the classroom. No textbook can contain the exact wisdom teachers require when dealing with a difficult situation and no motivational speaker can provide teachers with the advice they seek when they are faced with multitudes of seemingly unique and impossible circumstances.

You might have the credibility of a university degree, the enthusiasm inspired by professional development, and years of experience on which you can confidently rely. The humbling truth, however, is that although "by this time you ought to be teachers," every educator has one thing in common; a need for each other.

This profession has days that are, quite simply, impossible. You will have days that will break you, days that will have you crying on your desk, days where you could be heard swearing in your vehicle on the way home, and days that will leave you wondering if you chose the right career.

You did.

There is no career that has the potential for such lasting, eternal rewards than the legacy a teacher can leave the children in their classroom. But no one can reap those rewards and leave that legacy by attempting to go this profession alone. Not only is it too difficult, but there is too much at stake for teachers to assume that they can handle the hardships of this job in isolation.

Your well-being, and that of the students in the classroom, depends not only on your own talents and efforts in the classroom, but also in your humility in recognizing when they are not enough. That piece of paper you earned after spending four years in university allows you to teach; but it does not guarantee that you will never need to be taught. Indeed, when the classroom walls seem about to cave in, it is time to reflect on your need for "someone to teach you again the basic principles."

MENTORSHIP

The Oxford Languages' (2021) definition of a mentor as an "experienced and trusted advisor" certainly captures the essence of the word with language that reflects its significance.

This particular definition focuses on the mentor's *experience*, their understanding of various situations, their ability to say, "I've been there," and the wisdom they have gained through lived years of practice. This Oxford explanation also highlights the concept of *trust*. All the experience and wisdom in the world are of little value to anyone if the person sharing that wisdom is not trusted by those with whom they are sharing it. Mentorship must be built on a foundation of trust if the mentee is going to perceive the advice they are being given as credible and valuable.

Lastly, the word "advisor" emphasizes that the mentor's role is to share their insights and knowledge, with full awareness that their advice is intended only as a suggestion. Mentorship is not, and cannot be, a dictatorship. The trust that is crucial in establishing a mentor/mentee relationship will be broken if the advice provided comes from the mindset that the mentor's way is the only way. Rather than see their experience and wisdom as the *only* way, a trustworthy and effective mentor will see what they have to offer as just that—an offering. And regardless if that offering of advice is accepted or rejected, the mentor must respect that decision in order to maintain that trustful relationship.

When the mentee views the mentor's experience as credible and valuable, and implicitly trusts that their advice will help them develop and improve, then that relationship is one in which the mentee will flourish. When any one of these criteria are missing—experience, trust, and the philosophy of sharing advice—the mentorship attempt will not gain any traction nor provide the service for which it was intended.

THE NECESSARY INGREDIENT: WILLINGNESS

Understanding this definition of a mentor as an "experienced and trusted advisor" paints a picture of the implied relationship between the two participants. Yet what is missing from this definition is the most fundamental piece to successful mentorship: willingness.

Organizations, including schools, have attempted to capitalize on the potential of having veteran employees advise the more inexperienced staff through various mentorship programs. While this is a noble endeavor, the concern with this type of forced mentorship is that it does not always guarantee the mentee is interested in, or willing to take, the advice of their assigned mentor. Nor does it guarantee that the mentor is interested in the role of advisor or willing to share from their learned experiences. Unless the mentor is *willing* to volunteer their time and expertise and the mentee is *willing* to thoughtfully consider that which the mentor has to offer, mentorship is truly little more than lip service to an initiative that is not reaching its full potential.

Being willing to admit that you have limitations is the first step toward personal growth. Being willing to acknowledge that someone else may have the knowledge, understanding, and experience to help you surpass those limitations is the second step. The third step is being willing to make yourself vulnerable by admitting your need for help and seeking assistance. A willingness to trust the experience of the mentor is the fourth step in successful mentorship. The fifth and final step in ensuring a mentorship experience will have a profound impact on your personal development is your willingness to put into practice some of the advice offered by your mentor.

The *will* to get better, to improve, and to grow is perhaps the most significant and most powerful characteristic of any successful educator.

MENTORSHIP ILLUSTRATED

The power and necessity of this characteristic of willingness is perhaps best illustrated with a story of a coach who recognized her need for help, and the willingness of a mentor to share his valuable experience.

Although Molly had played softball in high school, it was never really her sport. Throughout her somewhat competitive days of playing the game, she usually managed not to embarrass herself on the field, but she was not passionate about the game and had rarely picked up her glove since high school except to play the odd slow-pitch tournament with a group of friends.

When her daughter fell in love with softball, however, and the girls in that age group needed a coach to take them to the next level and help them train to be competitive at provincial championships, Molly knew she had to step up. She also knew, unfortunately, that she was unprepared to offer any sage advice born from years' worth of personal experience playing the sport, so she did what any rookie coach would do. Molly logged on to YouTube.

While this strategy worked relatively well for coming up with a few drills, Molly was lacking many pieces of the coaching puzzle that could really help the girls develop. She did not know, for example, how to correct their batting technique. All she could remember from her days of playing was the coach telling her teammates to "get those elbows up." So, she repeated that foolish but seemingly wise-sounding mantra, and as a result ended up with a team full of chicken-winged batters who were not getting any better at hitting the ball. Molly also struggled with explaining plays and strategies and could not remember from her short stints at 3rd base how to instruct her team of girls to play the other positions.

As the season progressed, the girls practiced various catching and throwing drills that Molly had learned from YouTube, they determinedly swung their bats with "elbows up" . . . and they got really good at cheers. If you have never coached twelve-year-old girls on the ball diamonds, you have also likely never experienced the absurd level of enthusiasm that can possibly be put into belting out nonsensical cheers at the top of their lungs. Win or lose, these girls' commitment to team spirit was inspiring, and it reflected the fact that they were unaware their coach was struggling to figure out how to help them get better.

It was around mid-season when a veteran coach happened to walk by the diamond one day and saw Molly adjusting her batter's elbows ("up a little higher") during a hitting drill in which the other ten players on the field were spread out, picking dandelions and swatting mosquitoes. And he asked her if she wanted some assistance.

This seasoned coach is a legend in the community for his successful coaching portfolio. Between coaching hockey and ball his entire adult life, he has won more provincial titles than most could claim. His commitment to sport is second only to his commitment to the deeper foundation that has always been his motivation for being involved in athletics. He refers to this foundation, his purpose for coaching, as being in the "business of growing people." This man was now offering to share his wisdom and experience on the ball field to help Molly hone her girls' skills and, ultimately, to help her "grow" them as people.

"Do you want some assistance?" he asked.

Molly just about wept with relief.

From this mentor, Molly gained the foundational skills of being a softball coach. Her "elbows up" mantra gave way to a much more effective batting philosophy that Coach Jim had personally developed over the years and dubbed the "ABCs." Molly's uncertainty regarding coaching the positional play of any athlete who was not on third base grew into a tentative confidence in understanding the role of each player on the field. Her inability to turn the throwing and catching drills she found on YouTube into applicable strategies gradually developed along with the girls' skills into making plays and getting outs.

Molly learned so much about softball over the short season that you are likely expecting this story to conclude with a happy ending—a good old "underdog becomes the champion" type of finale.

While there is no doubt that it would have been nice for Molly and her team to come home with a season-ending gold medal around their necks, the reality is that although they made it out of the round robin and into playoffs, they were not skilled enough to defeat the teams who were further on their development journey than they were.

Well . . . they were not skilled enough *"yet,"* as Molly's mentor would always remind her. There is a lot of power in that three-letter word that she had come to recognize represents hope for kids and an attainable goal for which they can strive. Although the team was not skilled enough *yet* to beat the stronger teams, the girls and Molly sat and watched the playoff teams compete during the final championship, recognizing areas where they could grow and improve and the skills they would need to work on to be more competitive next year. Those conversations turned the "yet" into a practical reality with concrete steps toward an achievable goal.

The beauty of the season, and even the way it ended, was that the girls recognized in themselves how far they had come and where they were capable of going. And Molly could clearly reflect on her own growth as a coach.

Molly knew she owed a debt of gratitude to the local coach and mentor for his willingness to share his knowledge and expertise on the sport of softball with her and her team of girls. But even more importantly than that, she owed him for the wealth of wisdom to which she was exposed in that short period of time on what it truly means to be a *coach*. Helping kids develop skills as an athlete is one thing, a necessary thing. Helping kids develop skills as people—that might be the *only* thing that matters in the end. Very few kids you coach will ever make a living out of their athletics. But they can make a life out of the lessons they learn on the field, the court, the track, or wherever they might be competing.

Sports, and other pasttimes or activities, provide the opportunity for kids to learn the essential skills of living a successful life: respect and compassion for others, dedication and perseverance, work ethic and grit, how to win, and how to lose.

Like their physical skills, however, if players do not have a coach to correct their swing, adjust their stance, or fine tune their grip to improve their athletic ability, neither can their personal skills improve if they do not have a coach to teach them how to correct their attitude, adjust their perspective, or fine tune their values so they can see the larger picture. These life lessons, more than the physical skills themselves, are what coaching should be about.

Through Coach Jim's mentorship, Molly began to learn how to do this, how to check in with each girl regularly, how to find ways to use their unique set of skills to help the team, how to ensure that each player found success, how to build their capacity and understanding of "team" rather than just a group of individual athletes. These are the invaluable lessons she learned at the hands of one far wiser than she, a mentor she respected and trusted.

SEEK A MENTOR, BE A MENTOR

Molly's story reflects the importance of, and value in, finding a mentor in all facets of life. It is so easy to get caught in the daily routine of school life that teachers forget to challenge themselves, they fail to look outside the box for a different way of doing things, and they tend to revel in the comfort of familiarity. But when teachers humble themselves to the point of recognizing that there might be a different way—a better way—of doing something and seek someone whom they can trust to challenge their perceptions, beliefs, and actions, then they grow as people. And they get better.

Of equal importance to seeking a mentor is the lesson inherent in this for the students in your class. When they witness you actively "practicing what you preach" in the sense that you are admitting you do not know everything, that you are seeking to improve, and that you are willing to continue to learn from others, they will see the value in being willing to be mentored themselves. Too often pride gets in the way of growth. It is far more difficult to embrace humility, acknowledge limitations, and admit the need for help than it is to continue on the path of doing what you have always done.

Yet when a teacher's pride prevents them from improving their classroom practices, it also prevents them from improving their students' experiences in that classroom. And that is a shame, especially when "going it alone" also denies students the rich opportunity to witness their teacher modeling the beauty of life-long learning, personal and professional growth, and the intrinsic desire to improve. After all, is that not exactly what all teachers hope for their students? And if that is the goal of education, then how can a teacher model anything less?

Challenge yourself to seek a mentor in an area that you know, despite how much you would like to avoid acknowledging the fact, is a weakness. Know that you are not alone. You may be just beginning your career in the classroom and are overwhelmed with the number of areas in which you would like to improve your practice, and you may be a veteran teacher who believes you have all the answers.

Regardless of anyone's level of expertise and ability, every single educator has areas in which you can improve, both in your weaknesses and in your strengths. In fact, "there is greater opportunity in focusing to improve your strengths than there is to focus on improving your weaknesses. Highly successful people are not void of weaknesses but their capacity to gain from their strengths is what propels them to accomplish great things" (Miker n.d.). Do not hesitate to find a mentor who you can trust to challenge you to see things in a different way so that you can improve both your strengths and your weaknesses.

And on the flip side of that equation; do not hesitate to be a mentor either. Have confidence in what you have to offer, and then offer it to others who could use your help, your wisdom, and your experience. Molly would likely have never deigned to ask the local coach to mentor her in coaching softball; in fact, she would have cringed at the suggestion of asking a retired coach to volunteer even more of his time than he already has. But true to his nature of serving others, he saw a need and offered to help. And Molly and her girls benefitted. Be that mentor for someone else; recognize how your strengths can complement others' and humbly offer your assistance.

Molly's team did not come home with a gold medal around their necks that season. But the girls came home as better players, Molly as a better coach, and certainly all of them as better *people* for having had the experience. As mentor Coach Jim would say after every single practice,

"We got better today."

That is what teaching and learning should always be about. Desire to get better. Seek ways to improve. Be willing to learn from others.

And you will get better.

Chapter 8

A Model of Good Works

> *"Show yourself in all respects to be a model of good works, and in your teaching show integrity, dignity."*
>
> Titus 2:7

There is not much more frustrating than having to teach a student or work with a colleague who has a disproportionate sense of entitlement. The belligerence of students who feel they are "entitled" to better marks, more chances, and no consequences for being apathetic and the attitudes of colleagues who feel they are "entitled" to the best schedules, more prep time, and evenings off can create a dangerously poisonous school environment.

Yet as irritating and frustrating as this selfishly entitled behavior is to deal with in the classroom and in the school, there is one sense in which each person, student, or colleague deserves to be entitled. Teachers should be as equally passionate about ensuring entitlement in this regard as they are about squashing it in all the other contexts.

Respect.

Every student that walks into the classroom is *entitled* to the knowledge that when they pass through that classroom door, they are entering a space where they will be treated with respect.

The only way to guarantee every student will sense that comfort in knowing they are respected is if it is first modeled by their teacher. When the teacher consistently models integrity and dignity in all that they do, in every interaction they have with students and colleagues, and in every challenging situation, that consistency eventually becomes expected by students. And when that modeling of integrity and dignity is a standard practice of the teacher, and a standard to which students are held accountable in the classroom, it then becomes a standard practice for students.

Note that the word "practice" was used strategically here, with the deliberate intent of implying the meaning of the word as both a verb and a noun.

While it is relatively easy to vow to establish a *practice*, or routine, of respect in the classroom, it takes a great deal of commitment and perseverance to daily *practice* the consistent respect that will ultimately turn the classroom into a place of safety and comfort to which every student is entitled.

If the teacher explicitly preaches lessons of integrity and dignity but fails to put those same lessons into practice, students learn what is implicitly being taught instead—namely that they do not need to value each other or respect others' differences. The result of *that* lesson is a classroom that abounds with entitlement—selfish, self-seeking, and self-righteous entitlement. Yet when a teacher deliberately *models* the good works of integrity and dignity and intentionally *practices* the actions that convey a foundation of respect, then the classroom abounds with a different type of entitlement—one where students recognize that their peers, not themselves, are entitled to acts of unselfishness, self-giving, and selflessness.

A MODEL OF GOOD WORKS

There are many real-life models of good works from which to choose to illustrate *how* to practice integrity and dignity in the classroom. Yet Harper Lee's famous fictional character, Atticus Finch, from the classic novel *To Kill a Mockingbird*, presents a very simple, though eloquent, instruction that provides endless practical applications for practicing respect in the classroom.

Some would argue that there is no place for *To Kill a Mockingbird* in today's classroom; that Atticus Finch's character represents systemic racism where black people can only be rescued by the white man. Others would argue that the novel is a timeless classic, that the beauty of the writing, the depth of characters, and the lessons to be learned from the story are invaluable and still relevant in today's world. Regardless of which side of the argument you might be on, the point of discussing Atticus Finch's character in this chapter is not to debate the pros and cons of teaching the literary classic. Rather, it is to examine one of the lesser-known Atticus precepts that can help inform your classroom practice.

For those who may be unfamiliar with the epic novel, Atticus Finch is a lawyer and the single father of the main character, a young girl named Scout. Although a fictional and literary character, Atticus Finch epitomizes the qualities being studied in this chapter. He is a model of good works in his tenacious effort to fight against the racism in his community. In all his interactions, and particularly when he is teaching and parenting his children, he consistently demonstrates integrity and dignity. When treated with disrespect by those who disagree with him, Atticus steadily displays compassion and understanding rather than anger and offense.

At one point, Scout questions Atticus about why he feels compelled to defend a black man accused of raping a white woman when their entire community thinks he is wrong to do so. Atticus replies to her question with a phrase that does not get repeated nearly as often as some of this character's other nuggets of wisdom. Regardless of how familiar you are with the novel, there is a good chance you have heard some of the timeless advice Harper Lee dispels through this character, such as, "You never really understand a person until you consider things from his point of view . . . until you climb into his skin and walk around in it."

Atticus's response to Scout's question regarding his stubborn, and according to the community, ill-advised defense of the black man provides a firm foundation upon which the philosophy of a classroom can be built. He tells Scout that "they are certainly entitled to think that, and they are entitled to full respect for their opinions" (Lee 1988, 139).

Perhaps this particular quote has not become one of the more popularly spouted Atticus precepts because it challenges people and forces them to be uncomfortable. How many people, when they are in the middle of an argument, would be willing to take a step back and recognize that although they do not agree with the other's opinion, that person is still justified in expressing their point of view? And not only admit that they are justified in expressing this point of view, but are entitled to respect for that opinion?

It is not easy to concede that others' viewpoints might not only be legitimate but may also prove to be more insightful. It is particularly difficult to swallow the pride that sometimes prevents acknowledging when others are right. And when you passionately disagree with someone regarding a topic on which you are convinced you are right, it is almost impossible to do as Atticus suggests, and show respect for the other perspective.

"They are certainly entitled to think that, and they are entitled to full respect for their opinions." This quote bears repeating and a moment of reflection for how these words might challenge you in different situations. That particularly dreadful word "entitled" is used twice in this nugget of literary wisdom and yet the irony of that might make you smile. This is *exactly*, and perhaps the *only* thing people should be entitled to beyond the scope of basic human rights. Respect. One word, and yet the lack of it is the root of all sorts of evil in this world.

QUICK WRITES: A VEHICLE FOR TEACHING RESPECT

The character of Atticus Finch provides an understanding of how to practice integrity and dignity—by respecting the opinions of others. Exactly what that looks like in a classroom can be done in a variety of ways, but one practical example can be taken from an adaptation of Penny Kittle and Kelly Gallagher's idea of Quick Writes.

The basic idea with Quick Writes, although you can refer to Kittle's work, *Write Beside Them* (2008) for much more detailed information, is that you provide students with some type of prompt (e.g., quote, image, statistic, infographic, or news article) at the beginning of class and let them write without rules, structure, or judgment for 5 to 10 minutes. *Without judgment.* Yes, "without judgment" was already mentioned. But it needs to be emphasized because it is the most critical element to success in modeling respect for opinions.

Kittle and Gallagher model Quick Writing as a transparent process where students learn writing skills from watching you physically write on the screen as they also write. They developed it as a teaching tool to show students how to go back and revise, edit, and improve their writing. While this is an admirable and effective use of the Quick Write strategy, it can also be used to serve a different, and more expansive, purpose in the classroom environment.

Quick Writes is an effective tool in teaching the writing process, but more importantly, it can be used as an effective tool in the learning process to become a respectful human. In both processes, teaching writing and how to become respectful, the success of Quick Writes depends upon two things: your personal engagement in the process and your adeptness at choosing provocative prompts. If you buy into this routine as a teacher, physically engage in it with your students and personally grow from it as a person, then you are modeling exactly what you expect of your students. And when you model expectations, students tend to strive to meet them.

The other factor in ensuring success with Quick Writes in your classroom relies, in part, on your ability to choose the right topic. Choosing the right topic can be a daunting task when you consider the philosophy that this could become part of your daily classroom routine. It is unlikely that all your prompts will provoke earth-shattering written responses, but that is okay, because sometimes the topics you expect to be most engaging fall flat and others you assume will emit dry and boring responses are sometimes the most inciting.

Depending on your comfort level . . . actually scratch that comment. *Regardless* of your comfort level, choose the touchy topics. Do not shy away from the sensitive topics that might cause controversy or compel students to write things that you do not want to hear. These are the topics on which you *need* to hear from your kids. And just as importantly, these are the topics where they need to hear from you. For this Quick Write strategy to be effective in helping you model integrity and dignity, and therefore establishing the same standard for your students, you will need to be vulnerable when you write alongside your kids.

When you finish your Quick Write, read it out loud in class. If you are truly practicing vulnerability, there may be times when your own writing creates such a turmoil of sentiment within you that you know you will not get through it without displaying some of those emotions. Sometimes you may even have to ask a student to read your Quick Writes aloud for you because you know you will not be able to finish what you have written.

Yes, you are being encouraged in this chapter to be that vulnerable in front of your students. Be real, be vulnerable, and be transparent with them. Allow them to see your emotions and know your thoughts. The incredible beauty of allowing yourself to be that open with your students is that, in return, you will be gifted with their realness, their vulnerabilities, and their transparency. When you are honest with them, they will learn to trust that you will respect them if they are honest in return. And this is the crux of Atticus Finch's wisdom: "They are certainly entitled to think that, and they are entitled to full respect for their opinions."

This, above all else, is the classroom mantra that will allow students to feel comfortable in their entitlement to respect in your space. After you share your Quick Write thoughts, ask students if they are willing to share theirs. Depending on the group of kids, you may or may not get any volunteers. That is okay. Wait them out.

If you have a classroom competition of some sort going on (chapter 4: Sharpen Each Other), you may want to award points to their team for reading their Quick Writes out loud. Yes, that is admittedly shameless bribery, but to get students sharing their thoughts if they are initially hesitant to do so, you may need to do almost whatever it takes to get one or two students to read. It is *that* important that they do so if you are ever going to establish a routine of trust and respect in your classroom. Once a few students begin volunteering, you will soon notice the reading aloud of their Quick Writes becomes a habit in which others are willing to engage.

After the student volunteers finish reading, thank them for doing so, without any judgment on their shared perspective, and then ask the class if anyone had a different opinion. Now here is where it can get dicey and where people may shy away from this activity. Do you really want opinionated students in your classroom going head to head on different topics that are not superficial? Do you want to allow kids the opportunity to debate the subjects that get them fired up, the topics that matter most, the controversial themes that hit them where they are in their journey to adulthood?

Yes! Yes, you want this. You want this debate in your classroom because this is where the best learning happens, when students learn from each other. But first and foremost, the entitlement of full respect for opinions *MUST* be established. Kids must learn, know, and *trust*, that they are safe in your classroom and safe with each other. And they can only learn that if you first model the respect that you expect them to have for each other.

This means that when a student shares a Quick Write that is particularly inflammatory and entirely against what you stand for and believe in, you still need to demonstrate respect for them as people, even when you completely disagree with their opinion. Teachers encounter every perspective, belief, and value system that this world has to offer in the melting pot of a classroom. These kids come from every background imaginable and represent a vast array of diverse family experiences and values. When they express a belief that is contrary to what you value, if you do not first respect that belief and its origin, you will lose that child's trust and respect.

You cannot, and will never, effectively inspire a student to rethink their potentially provoking belief by telling them they are wrong because, in essence, that is equal to telling them their family is wrong, that their way of life is wrong, and that the foundation on which they have been raised is wrong. If you were to do this, you will lose any opportunity you may have to challenge them to think differently, to show them another side to the argument, and potentially to shift their thinking in a way it would not if you quell that chance by disrespecting their point of view in the first place.

QUICK WRITES: WHEN IT GETS UNCOMFORTABLE

You can well imagine that if you implement the suggestions provided thus far in this chapter, things are bound to get uncomfortable in your classroom. You are not wrong. Yet unfortunately when the topics that are the most difficult to address are deliberately avoided in the classroom, educators are implicitly teaching students they are not appropriate subjects for conversation. The reality is, avoiding discomfort in the classroom does not mean that you are ensuring kids will never have those controversial conversations. It only means that those discussions will occur in a space that is not supervised by a caring adult and in a place where respect is not the underlying foundation.

Mr. G is an educator who firmly believes in allowing his students freedom of expression in the classroom. One afternoon, however, a student's right to this freedom of opinion infringed on the right his peers had to feel respected. When these freedoms collide, which is inevitable in a classroom that encourages students to express their opinions, teachers must be prepared to respond. Mr. G had two choices in this incident: he could have dealt with the disrespectful student's use of his freedom of expression in a manner that alienated that student, or he could have responded in a way that re-established the foundation of respect to which every student is entitled.

When Todd offered to share his Quick Write, Mr. G encouraged him with a smile, happy to have this normally reticent student volunteer. Mr. G was not expecting, however, for Todd to take the innocent daily prompt and turn it into an opportunity to share his opinion that "gay people's love for each other is unnatural, not as God intended in the Bible, and that they are a 'waste of skin.'"

Before Mr. G could halt Todd's hateful diatribe, the damage had already been done, and the face of a peer in Todd's class, who everyone knew was transgendered, turned every shade of red to white as they experienced the horror, embarrassment, and shame that resulted from Todd's words.

What was the right thing to do in that situation? Should Mr. G have taken this Quick Write to the principal and had Todd suspended for his discriminatory beliefs? Should Mr. G have forced this student to publicly apologize to the class for expressing such unacceptable and prejudiced thoughts?

Those were certainly options available to Mr. G, and suggestions that he knew he would probably get if he were to ask for advice. But Mr. G did neither of those things. Knowing that this student's belief stemmed from a staunchly conservative and religious upbringing, he did not want to immediately denounce these beliefs fostered by Todd's family that he felt compelled, and respected enough in the classroom, to share.

But neither does Todd's upbringing justify him telling other students in his class that they are "unnatural" and a "waste of skin." Like good old Atticus, no teacher should ever tolerate injustice or discrimination of any form in their classroom. The emotions on that young transgendered student's face make it clear why tolerance of injustice can lead to horrific consequences.

But Mr. G also knew that if he publicly maligned the student who had expressed those opinions, gave him consequences for sharing his beliefs, and shamed him for voicing his thoughts, he would have lost any and all chance of reaching this student, not to mention the precedent he would be setting for other students who would from then on be afraid to share their personal thoughts out of fear of his reaction.

This is a very fine line to walk, an almost impossible balance to find. To facilitate true understanding of each other, true learning to happen, and true respect to evolve, somehow teachers must find a way to encourage kids to feel comfortable expressing their inner thoughts and reflections without fear of judgment, and yet get them to do so without making their classmates feel like they are, for lack of a better phrase, "a waste of skin."

Knowing he could have avoided this whole situation by having proofread the Quick Writes first himself and only asking for certain students to volunteer their responses, by having given a superficial and unprovoking Quick Write topic, or by simply not engaging in the routine of Quick Writes in the first place, Mr. G exasperatedly shook off his self-recriminations and proceeded to embrace this situation for what it was—an opportunity to learn from each other.

So, here's what Mr. G did do. You could certainly argue that his actions were not the right response, and they are definitely not the only solution in this situation. Maybe he should have hauled this student out by the ear and marched him right down to the office. Or maybe what Mr. G did was okay too.

"Todd," Mr. G began, "thanks for sharing your Quick Write today." The class was silent. As in the metaphorical pin-drop silent. Everyone was waiting for Mr. G's reaction to such an inflammatory response and his habitual response of "thanking" a student for volunteering to share their thoughts was unexpected in this volatile situation. Mr. G looked around the room and addressed the elephant head on. "I know you are all waiting to hear what I am going to say to him because you are probably as shocked as I am that something like that just got read out loud." Some students nervously chuckled at this admission, unsure of where he was going.

"Here's the thing. You guys know and have heard me repeat it often, and have hopefully seen me live it enough, to know that I mean it when I say that everyone is entitled to respect for their opinions. Everyone. But if you want respect for your opinion, it is a two-way street. You must also respect others. And I want you all to consider what respecting others looks like in this circumstance that we find ourselves in today. You may expect to be respected for your beliefs in this classroom, BUT, that entitlement only works if you likewise demonstrate respect for others."

"Todd," and Mr. G deliberately made eye contact with him, "I have more to say to you. You'll read it in your journal later, but I think you know that this conversation is not finished." Seeing Todd nod in affirmation and noting the absence of a cocky smirk on his face, Mr. G recognized with relief that Todd was already thinking seriously about his actions.

Mr. G gathered the Quick Write journals, changed the topic, and quickly got the class working on the next part of the day's lesson. He was not satisfied with how he had handled the situation and, as he had said to Todd, knew that the conversation was not finished. Mr. G took the journals home, as was his habit, and replied in writing to the kids' responses for the day.

If you decide to try and implement the Quick Write habit in your classroom, take advantage of the opportunity to get to know the kids through their writing and make sure they feel like they have been heard by seeing your personal handwritten responses. Your responses can be as varied as their initial writing. You may just offer a quick comment or "thanks for making me think" about the topic of the day. You may pose a question to them for clarification or to challenge them to think about something in a different way. Your replies might sometimes initiate further conversation through their journals that you would not necessarily have with the kids if you had not established that medium for communication.

Yes, this process takes time and is burdensome for teachers who employ this routine with multiple classes of students. But it is time very well spent and is always well worth the effort. Students will tell you that they look forward to getting their journals back and reading your comments because to them it means someone took the time to really listen to what they felt compelled to say, which in turn makes them feel comfortable and willing to share again the next time they write. Although the Quick Write journals were intended by Kittle and Gallagher as a tool for teaching and modeling the writing process, they can also be used as an irreplaceable tool to simply communicate with your kids.

Mr. G took those Quick Write journals home that evening and deliberately left two journals to the end. He addressed the transgendered student first. This student's entry was innocuously innocent, having taken the suggested topic in a completely different direction than the other accusatory student had. Mr. G wrote a compassionate note and expressed his respect for their strength in living in a society where judgment seems inevitable and regret that they were exposed to such blatant judgment in the classroom where he had sought to promote respect and understanding. Mr. G closed by stating that they were welcome to come to him with any thoughts or concerns, either through their writing or with a personal visit to his classroom.

Mr. G saved Todd's journal for last. Again, he knew from where this student's beliefs stemmed. To tell Todd that his beliefs are wrong is to tell him that his parents are wrong, that how he was raised is wrong, that the underlying foundation of faith that has guided his family for generations is wrong. Who was Mr. G to do that to a child? Is that his place as an educator? And yet as the teacher who is striving to find that balance in the classroom, it is absolutely Mr. G's place to ensure that while this student feels respected *for* his opinion, he must also be taught to ensure others feel that same level of respect *from* him.

Mr. G knew this student well and actually predicted that when he made the general statement about "gay" people, he was not thinking of the specific names of peers sitting in his classroom. Is that not often the case with any type of discrimination? It is relatively easy to believe certain things about a group of people, but when faced with the unique identity of any one of those people who do not necessarily fit the given "mold," it makes you question the stereotypes that had been ascribed to the entire group.

Mr. G picked up his pen and responded to Todd's Quick Write response that he had read aloud in class that day.

"While I always appreciate hearing your Quick Write responses, Todd, today's response offers both of us an opportunity to learn something. When we ascribe a general feeling about a group to individuals within the group, does it hold true? For example, when you said in general that gay people are 'a waste of skin,' would you still be comfortable saying that to the face of each of your classmates? Those kids in your classroom felt condemned by you today. They did not feel respected for who they are. While I want to ensure you feel respected for your opinions, I also have the same obligation to guarantee your classmates feel respected for theirs. You took that away from them today, and that is unacceptable in this class."

Mr. G was anxious about the next day's Quick Writes and knew that he had a choice. He could post a completely unrelated topic that would avoid the issue the class had faced yesterday, but he could not convince himself to take the coward's way out of dealing with this topic head on. Mr. G felt like his students would expect more from him. He considered posting a simple "what does respect in the classroom look like?" type of question but felt that was a somewhat elementary type of teacher strategy and he did not want the kids to feel like they were being talked down to after the seriousness of yesterday's incident.

Mr. G chose instead to open the class with the following quote from a past Canadian prime minister, John Diefenbaker: "I am a Canadian, free to speak without fear, free to worship in my own way, free to stand for what I think right, free to oppose what I believe wrong, or free to choose those who shall govern my country. This heritage of freedom I pledge to uphold for myself and all mankind."

Before he let them begin writing, Mr. G read the quote out loud, and the class talked briefly about its meaning. He told them he thought Diefenbaker and Atticus would likely get along really well, as long as Diefenbaker amended his quote to say, "free to do all of these things while respecting these same freedoms for others."

Some of the students chuckled and rolled their eyes at Mr. G's persistence in finding ways to fit his classroom mantra into every aspect of the class, but the point was made. He then asked them to consider which freedoms from Diefenbaker's list they have enjoyed, which freedoms they felt had been infringed upon, and lastly to try to come up with an example of each one of those freedoms in their lives.

In true teenage style, as you might imagine, the students gave all sorts of responses. Some kids took the prompt lightly and wrote about their parents imposing consequences for breaking curfew as an infringement on their freedoms. Some kids took it very literally and cited different ways they had experienced each one of the freedoms on the list. A couple of kids responded by referring to yesterday's incident and simply said that they thought although Todd has the freedom to express his beliefs, that freedom should be denied when it causes harm to someone or infringes on someone else's freedoms.

One student's response had Mr. G sit back in his chair later that evening as he read through the stack of Quick Write books. Settling in to re-read, Mr. G paused to appreciate the depth and maturity of the thoughts of this student.

> As teenagers, we have these freedoms that Diefenbaker listed, gifts that were earned for us by people we do not know and will never meet. These freedoms were fought for, died for, and won, by people who believed in the future of this country, and in us as the generation that would continue to build this nation.
>
> We have these freedoms and yet we will never truly understand the sacrifice that was made to earn them. Answering this Quick Write by listing my freedoms makes me feel like a kid at Christmas who can recite the gifts I received, gifts that I'm not even sure I wanted, don't believe I need, and do not appreciate the time, thought or money that went into their purchase. But then, like any spoiled kid, I get angry with jealousy when my sibling wants to borrow this gift that I did not want, need, or appreciate, let alone earn.
>
> Our freedoms are like that. We don't even know we want or need them. We don't appreciate the sacrifice that went into earning them, but then we make sure if someone tries to take them from us, we fight to keep them, and in the process, deny others those same freedoms.
>
> Maybe instead of abusing our freedoms and taking them for granted, we can use them as was intended by those who earned them for us and ensure they are upheld for ALL mankind, regardless of who we are, what we look like, or our sexual orientation.

And just like that, Mr. G recognized he was blessed to have a real-life Atticus Finch in his classroom.

Mr. G anonymously read this Quick Write aloud in class the next day and, like the silence the day before, you could have heard a pin drop in the room when he finished. But this time, it was not a silence of apprehension. It was a silence of reverence and respect for the light that had been cast on a topic that had been fraught with tension. When Mr. G was done reading, Todd spoke up, hesitantly and quietly. "I took my freedom of expression for granted yesterday. I realize what I said took away other people's right to be respected. And I'm sorry."

For teachers, these are the moments where you are mere instruments of a greater education being taught. An education that is beyond textbooks and curriculum. An education that strikes each soul in the room . . . and makes each one better.

What a gift.

Chapter 9

Honor Everyone

"Honor everyone. Love the brothers and sisters. Honor the emperor."

1 Peter 2:17

Scrolling through the feed of any politician's social media accounts is enough to make one question where the critically vocal comment-writers were the day their parents or teacher told them, "If you don't have anything nice to say, don't say anything at all." For those with undaunted keyboard courage, the relative anonymity of the internet has provided them a safe forum to spew their hatred and venom, unleashing the depth of their bitterness on anyone who happens to scroll down the list of comments. Sadly, the old-fashioned ideas of honor and love that are presented in this chapter's verse seem to have no place in political social media forums.

Living in today's world where social media threatens the sanity of the normal user is challenging enough but imagine being a politician during these times where every word you say is captured for eternity, and then scrutinized, debated, and ripped apart by a condemning populace who would never want to do the job themselves, but are very quick to make it clear that they could do it better. Unfortunately, the unfiltered mudslinging on platforms such as Facebook, Twitter, or Instagram has become such a socially accepted method of expressing political alliances that this expectation of being able to say whatever one wants has slowly crept into the place where such partisan beliefs have no place: the classroom.

The derogatory comments, insulting mockery and defamation of political leaders might be considered appropriate in many venues and has obviously (perhaps shamefully) become the manner in which people claim their right to freedom of expression on social media, but if you are trying to instill a culture of respect in your classroom, allowing these kinds of conversations is hypocritically practicing the opposite of what you are preaching. In a classroom where you are establishing a foundation of respect for people's differences, including their political points of view, "honor everyone" must be the practice to which you resort when these differences arise.

That does not mean, however, that politics do not have a place in the classroom. On the contrary. The classroom is the ideal environment to begin teaching the next generation of voters, politicians, and citizens about government and democratic ideals. And it is the perfect place to model for students how to honor *everyone*, including the "emperor," president, prime minister, governor, premier, or whomever holds political office, even if you did not vote for them.

Teachers have a unique opportunity to foster democratic characteristics in tomorrow's youth by establishing relationships with students, allowing them voice and advocacy, and most importantly, respecting students' perspectives and contributions in discussions. When teachers model democratic values and consistent respect, the classroom becomes a space where those values can flourish in practical and realistic ways, which is undeniably the best way for students to learn the philosophy of democracy.

Unfortunately, however, rather than modeling respect for both sides of the political spectrum and demonstrating the underlying principles of democracy, many teachers use the classroom in ways that mimic a social media platform and take advantage of the opportunity the classroom presents to push their own agendas.

A thread of comments on a politician's Facebook feed reflects the public's perception that classrooms have, indeed, become avenues for teaching political ideology. The thread began with an exasperated parent lambasting teachers for "indoctrinating our children with left-wing beliefs," to which someone else responded, "oh, so it's not ok to indoctrinate children with left-wing politics but it's ok for teachers to turn our kids into right-wing radicals"?

The world will always be divided between left-and right-wing politics, with people scattered everywhere throughout the spectrum. And that is as it should be. The only way to hold a left-or right-wing government accountable is to have the opposition continuously challenge the beliefs and actions of the governing party. This opposition ensures there are checks and balances that keep a government from having too much control and from making decisions that do not reflect the needs of the general populace. The system is not without flaws, but it is a system that successfully continues to govern first world countries without war, famine, or poverty, so despite its imperfections, it seems to work.

Perhaps ironically, classrooms do not always operate with the same systems of checks and balances as a parliamentary or congressional forum. Unchecked, a teacher's political beliefs can be used, as the Facebook commentators angrily observed, to indoctrinate children to believe a certain way.

Often the only adult in the classroom, a teacher has the potential to use their influence to shape young minds and mold youths' beliefs into whatever they value. While this has incredible power to positively influence the next generation of children, it also has the unnerving power to leave students with the impression there is only one side to the political debate.

Teachers by default have what most politicians desire—a captive audience—who has been taught from the first day of kindergarten to respect and listen to their teacher. In most other settings, when the discussion turns to politics, people have the option of engaging in, or walking away from, the conversation. Students do not enjoy that same freedom of choice as they are required to be in attendance during class. When teachers take advantage of that class time to push their own agenda, students are left with no alternative other than to listen. They have no alternative, that is, unless the teacher provides them with one.

Deliberately including politics in the classroom should be as much about teaching students about politics as it should be about teaching them how to *discuss* politics, according to Hess and McAvoy, authors of *The Political Classroom* (2014). As with most topics, kids come into the classroom with many preformed notions and opinions based on a variety of contexts including their family's beliefs, cultural norms, and peer pressures. Rather than try to convince students those pre-conceived beliefs are wrong, teachers can foster open and honest discussion about why those beliefs exist, why others might believe differently, and most importantly, how people with opposing beliefs can live harmoniously.

In this digital age, students have more access to news and are more informed on current events than any previous generation of youth. Not only are they privy to massive amounts of information, but they are also inundated with opinions on every topic that might pop up in the media. As a result, students often come into classrooms believing themselves to be experts on a subject, having gained their "knowledge" from various questionable sources.

Teachers have choices in these situations when students arrive to class, heatedly discussing the most recent controversial political decision. Educators can choose to take advantage of these opportunities to preach their beliefs about one side of the issue, or they can use them to preach instead about how to consider both sides of the story. Even more importantly, and with longer-lasting implications for the future, teachers can also use current events to teach critical viewing, listening, and reading skills. They can show students how to examine news, social media posts, and advertisements for bias and prejudice.

In teaching students how to see issues from multiple perspectives, as well as to critically examine and question the source and presentation of the information with which they are constantly bombarded, students can also be taught a lesson most people would, unfortunately, prefer not to learn. Politics in the classroom provides the opportunity to teach students about honor: "Honor everyone. Love the brothers and sisters. Honor the emperor" (1 Peter 2:17).

When it comes to politics, honor is typically one of the furthest virtues from the electorate's minds. After all, when you watch the disrespectful, insulting, and bullying political debates on television and observe the nasty campaign rhetoric during pre-election season, it is difficult to find honorable behaviour anywhere. Post-election times are not any better as most politicians continue to treat their opponents with manners that would be considered deplorable in any other social situation. Citizens who are caught up in the emotional arguments of political parties tend to follow suit and view anyone with opposing beliefs as uninformed, unintelligent, and unworthy of respect.

This obstinate refusal to not only listen to the other side, but also to fail to treat them with respect, are not the true democratic ideals upon which this country was found. Educators, however, can combat the dishonor that seems to characterize politics by teaching their students to become informed, by challenging them to use their intelligence, and by expecting them to respect others' views. In putting these democratic characteristics into practice, educators are showing students what it looks like to *honor* others.

When teachers model what it means to honor others in the classroom, it does not mean that they are teaching students to believe as they do. Rather, teaching kids to honor others means explaining that they are free to disagree with each others' different beliefs, views, and political allegiances, but that they must respect each other for those differences. As challenging, impossible, and uncomfortable though it might be for some teachers, the best way to teach students about honor is to model it in situations where you are most reluctant to do so.

CLASSROOM STUDY 1: POLITICAL SOAPBOX

Mr. W was newly hired to teach in a very conservative community. Very quickly, it became apparent that his vocal liberal beliefs were not common, nor popular, within the school community. He made no secret of his disgust for what he perceived to be the incompetent and immoral leadership of the conservative government, and likewise made no secret of his intolerance for those who would vote for such a "corrupt" leader.

Mr. W's classroom routine included daily perusal of headlines for material he could use as evidence to support his assessment of the government's ineptitude. Not only were these articles presented to the students with this biased lens, but anyone who dared to disagree with Mr. W was told they were wrong and made to feel very foolish.

It did not take very long for Mr. W's method of humiliating students in class and mocking their belief system to make students averse not only to his teaching methods, but also to his political views. Rather than convincing the students to consider issues and events from a liberal perspective, Mr. W's blatant criticism of the conservative government many of his students' families had voted for, served to alienate them and reinforce their beliefs that liberal philosophy was wrong.

Kale, a senior student in Mr. W's social science class, had grown sick of hearing how anyone with conservative views were close-minded, redneck, racist, and ignorant. Although his family had always taught him to respect others' views, he could muster no respect for this teacher who was continually "shoving his beliefs down our throat," as the kids in his class said. In one particularly challenging conversation, Kale tried to explain to Mr. W how an imposed carbon tax would negatively affect his family's agricultural operation.

"It's people like you who are ruining the environment for the next generation," Mr. W exploded in response to Kale's explanation. "People like you have no respect for those of us who actually care about the planet and other people."

"'People like us?'" Kale retorted with exasperation. "'People like us' actually work the land and do everything we can to protect it. 'People like us' don't just sit back and enjoy the products of other people's hard work, meanwhile criticizing how they work. You seem to like your sandwiches every day for lunch but have you ever had to work to produce the flour that makes your bread? I've seen you enjoy burgers at our school's hamburger sales, but have you ever actually got up at 6:00 in the morning to feed a herd in the middle of the freezing cold winter?

"Yes, our combines and tractors burn fossil fuels. And it's true that fossil fuels aren't perfect. But imposing a carbon tax when there is no alternative to fossil fuels in agriculture makes it almost impossible for 'people like us' to produce that bread and those burgers you seem to enjoy. I'm sick of listening to you criticize 'people like us' when you know NOTHING about us." With that last statement, Kale stormed out of the classroom, slamming the door behind him.

Sputtering with anger over Kale's outburst, Mr. W snapped at the class. "That is *exactly* the kind of attitude that is ruining our earth. Now let's forget about that ignorant little rant you just heard and move on with today's lesson." Ignoring the rolled eyes and shared looks of irritation among the students, Mr. W continued as though nothing had happened.

Despite the students' frustration with Mr. W's use of the classroom as his own personal political soapbox, he was not called to task for his biased teaching until he ultimately crossed a line. The day Mr. W was caught scraping the decal of the conservative party off Kale's truck in retaliation for Kale's constant challenging of his political views was the day Mr. W was suspended from his job.

CLASSROOM STUDY 2: POLITICAL PERSPECTIVES

In another classroom, Mr. G is also a proud, card-carrying member of the liberal political party. Mr. G attends every rally he can, supports his party by volunteering during election campaigns, and makes no secret of his political beliefs in the classroom. Although his students know him to be a staunch liberal supporter, they also know *why* he believes as he does. Mr. G consistently presents his political philosophies and beliefs regarding the government's handling of current events, but then always invites debate regarding these topics. He encourages students to argue with him, to find evidence to support their point of view, and to critically question his own supporting arguments.

Mr. G was particularly critical of what he perceived to be the conservative government's lack of concern regarding, and unwillingness to act on, the increasing unemployment rate. To get the conversation flowing, he provided an article for his students to read that presented statistics and data on the number of people who were without work and the ramifications of unemployment on individuals as well as the country.

After reading the article, Kelly shyly raised her hand. She was not typically a vocal student and was hesitant to contradict or question her teacher, but she had quietly observed that when other students challenged Mr. G on several occasions, he never appeared angry but rather seemed pleased that they had shared their differing opinions. Having witnessed Mr. G's habitual respect of contradictory points of view gave her the courage to slowly raise her hand and speak cautiously, yet confidently, when Mr. G called upon her.

"This article definitely makes unemployment seem like a big problem, Mr. G, and I'm not saying that it isn't. But I can't help but wonder about two things. First, the author of this article is the opposition critic for social services so obviously she is presenting a biased point of view. Second, probably because it's her role to be critical, she deliberately doesn't even list any examples of what the government is doing to counter unemployment. I did a quick search on my phone and found a long list of programs that the government has in place to try and help people find jobs. So even though the stats look bad, it's not like the government isn't doing anything.

"I think her argument might have more merit if she acknowledged what the government is doing and then provided some research to say why those programs are ineffective and offered alternative solutions."

Mr. G crossed his arms, leaned back on the stool upon which he sat at the front of the classroom, and grinned.

"Kelly," he stated, pride evident in his voice, "thank you for speaking up today. You make some great points. We have talked often about biased reporting and I'm glad to see that lesson has sunk in and that you recognized the author's prejudiced perspective. I'm impressed that you thought to question the author's role in government and understand how that would affect her presentation of the information. I'm also impressed that you thought of another way she could have addressed this issue. So impressed, in fact, that we are going to make that today's task. Grab your computers, folks, and let's get to work. What is the government doing to combat unemployment? Let's compile a list and then discuss what we find."

Students were quick to get engaged in the lesson of the day, which was originally spurred on by the teacher's personal political perspective that unemployment was the government's fault, but that had evolved through his willingness to listen to, and respect, his students' perspectives. Not only did this lesson provide Mr. G's students with authentic learning regarding biased reporting and actions that can be taken to counter unemployment rates, but it also provided them with a more significant and memorable lesson on democracy as they witnessed Mr. G put into practice the democratic values that he was always preaching.

POLITICS HAS A PLACE

Mr. G's approach to teaching politics in the classroom is undeniably preferable to that of Mr. W for many reasons. Rather than castigating his students for defying him, Mr. G compliments students on their application of the critical thinking skills he had been teaching them in class. Instead of forcing his points of view upon the class, he is open to allowing the lesson to move in whatever direction their perspectives take the discussion.

Most significantly, although Mr. G openly disagrees with the government's approach to national and international affairs, he never maligns the leader as a person, nor does he mock and insult those who align themselves with a particular politician's beliefs. Choosing instead to practice the value of "honor" that he is trying to instill in his students, Mr. G will acknowledge the reasons behind the government's decisions and explain how they align with the philosophy of a conservative party. Then he might jokingly explain what he would have done differently if the leader of the governing party had asked his opinion, and the class engages in that humor, knowing he is presenting two sides to the issue as well as using self-deprecation to make them laugh.

Teachers should not be expected to hide their own political beliefs, but they should be expected not to use them to indoctrinate children to believe as they do. Teaching students how to honor others' opinions, and how to honor the current governing party, is challenging when you do not agree with, or possibly even respect, the leader's actions and decisions. Yet the fact remains that in a democracy, the governing party is elected into leadership and teaching students to honor the democratic system has more positive potential for society as a whole than teaching them to hate their leader.

If you can overcome the challenge of wanting to persuade students to believe as you do, they will learn much more about the building blocks of a democratic society than if you insist they see things your way. Be authentic and real; there is no need to pretend to believe differently than you do. In fact, if students know that you are a passionate conservative, for example, but demonstrate respect for the liberal party's leader, the lesson of honor is much more effectively modeled than if you use your classroom as a soapbox to preach only one point of view, insincerely try to remain neutral, or worse, avoid the issue of politics altogether.

HONOR EVERYONE

The captive audience of the students in the classroom offers teachers the powerful opportunity to not only preach about the democratic values upon which this country was built, but to practice them in *every* interaction, even those with political undertones. Recent political upheavals regarding racial tensions, gun control, welfare and universal basic income, LGBTQ+ rights, and so much more, are unavoidable when they are the lived realities of the students in the classroom.

Because these sensitive political topics are the daily experiences of the students in the classroom, they must therefore also be the topics of classroom conversations. Teachers are fooling themselves if they assume that avoiding these discussions in the classroom means that students will not engage in them on their own. Providing a safe place for students to have structured and disciplined conversations about these difficult topics will teach them to honor each other's views, and the reasons for these views, if doing so is first modeled by the teacher.

Politics are inevitable in the classroom. Students' lives are affected by political decisions and in a democratic country, they have the right to have an opinion on the issues that have the potential to change their lives. Teachers also have the right to have an opinion and should not be expected to leave that opinion at the classroom door when they arrive at work. Rather, they can use their opinions to model for students what it looks like to firmly believe in one side, support those beliefs with credible evidence, and yet be open to discussion and debate by those who disagree. And most importantly, teachers can then model what it looks like to *honor* those with whom they disagree.

This is the power of politics in the classroom; not the opportunity the captive audience provides teachers to indoctrinate children to "their" side, but rather the opportunity it provides teachers to indoctrinate children to honor "everyone's" side.

Chapter 10

For the Rights of All

"Open your mouth for the mute, for the rights of all who are destitute. Open your mouth, judge righteously, defend the rights of the poor and needy."

Proverbs 31: 8–9

Kids are always worth your effort and your persistence. Even when they are hurting so badly that their pain causes them to lash out and hurt you, it is possible to look beyond their behavior to find the precious souls within who need your love, and because of that, it is possible to overlook and forgive their intended offense.

Although it is possible to overlook and forgive the hurt caused by students, sometimes it is more difficult to do so when that sense of hurt and betrayal is caused by the system in which you work.

When organizational leaders believe themselves infallible and their decisions foolproof, despite the voices crying out for change, people get hurt. In other businesses or organizations, the conceit of CEOs who believe they are the only ones who know best might negatively affect company culture and the financial bottom line. In an educational system, however, the bottom line that is affected is much more valuable, vulnerable, and significant. The bottom line in a school system is the children.

When the well-being of students is at stake, arrogance has no place in the leadership of an educational organization. Organizations of any kind are best governed by people who are willing to humble themselves to admit they do not always know best, and this is particularly true for leaders of education systems. The most effective leaders understand the value in listening to those who are working at the ground level, those who are most affected by the decisions made by a leadership that is often removed from the day-to-day grind of the organization.

In education, effective leadership means school district administration should be present in schools to witness the effects of their decisions. They should not only be willing to listen to those who are required to live with the practices forced upon them, but they should be actively and intentionally seeking the feedback of those whom they are hired to serve—students, parents, and communities.

When educational leaders place more value in their own opinions or in philosophical theory than the voices of those who are living the daily classroom reality, the result is rarely what is best for students.

The unfortunate truth is that often decisions are made regarding programming, staffing, spending, and the list could go on endlessly, that are completely out of your control as an educator, decisions you *know* will not only fail to help kids but may actually hurt them. These questionable decisions, policies and practices are often couched in language intended to deceive and portray an illusion of systemic success, but when examined closely, reveal concerning long-term effects on those who have no say in these decisions: the children.

You will often feel powerless to stop the runaway train that carries a cargo of policies and procedures that are based on theory or the desired illusion of success but are certainly not based on the reality you see in your classroom. But there is the catch. You may *feel* powerless, but be assured that you are not, indeed, without the ability to make a difference. It is in these situations that you are called upon to be an advocate for what is right and best for kids and to "open your mouth to . . . defend the rights" (Proverbs 31) of those who cannot speak for themselves.

WHEN THE SYSTEM FAILS KIDS

Josh was a grade two student with a December birthday. His parents hesitantly weighed the pros and cons the year he could have enrolled in kindergarten and decided that despite his late birthday, he seemed ready to begin his education at the age of four. He enjoyed kindergarten and playing with his friends, but despite his pleasure in attending school, the kindergarten teacher expressed some concern over his lack of reading-readiness by the time June rolled around. Josh's parents promised themselves they would work with him over the summer to get him ready for grade one, but as summer often does, it sped by without a great deal of time given to their vow.

Fast forward through a frustrating grade one year where Josh's earlier love of school was slowly chiseled away by his frustration with his inability to meet the more structured demands of a grade one classroom to the August before he would begin grade two. Josh's parents recognized they may have made a mistake by enrolling Josh in kindergarten when he was four and have chosen to request that he repeat grade one to help him catch up on the skills he did not achieve the previous year.

Additionally, Josh seems to be socially more at the same developmental age as the students going into grade one as he has gravitated to kids in that group on the playground and at the park over the past year. Socially and academically, Josh's parents are certain that retention is in his favor. As they sit in the principal's office and delineate these reasons for their request, they are astonished when they are told "no."

"Due to school district policy, a child cannot be held back," they were told. Shocked and furious, they explained that this was their choice, a decision they had labored over as parents and felt good about for their son's sake.

"I understand your position," the principal explained, "and I am sorry. But in the long term, you'll see that this is the right decision for Josh. The research shows that retention hurts kids more, especially socially, than it helps them."

Horrified and angry, Josh's parents left that meeting doubting themselves for their decision, the principal for his obstinacy, and the education system in general. They questioned who was in the better position to know what was best for their child—them, as his parents or educational research conducted by people who had never met their son Josh?

Years later, Josh's lack of academic success and constant social struggles led to drug abuse, dropping out of school, and an adulthood that began with regret rather than promise. Would all of this have been avoided if Josh's parents were granted their wish to have their son held back in elementary school? That is impossible to know. There are certainly case studies that provide examples of the alternate side of this argument, that students who were retained turned to drugs and poor choices due to their shame in being held back.

The point is, every student deserves to be considered as an individual rather than as a pawn in an unproven educational philosophy. Although it would definitely make education systems easier to manage if a "one size fits all" approach actually worked, anyone who has worked in a classroom is well aware that children rarely fit a mold that would make this approach successful.

Josh's story should in no way be interpreted as a commentary on enrolling late-birthday kids too early. Many of these students have been academically and socially successful attending school with their birth-year peers. Rather, this based-on-a-true story is a commentary on the consequences of following a policy to the letter without leaving room for individual consideration. Josh was deprived of an opportunity to foster friendships with kids who were at the same developmental level as he was and to build a foundation of academic skills by a policy that fails to consider "failure" as an option that leads to success.

Unbeknownst to Josh's parents, it was not just research upon which this rigid social promotion philosophy was based, but also on the school district's goal to improve their graduation rates. Students are tracked from elementary to high school and, in this particular district, graduation rates were based on students' ability to graduate with their kindergarten cohorts. Kids like Josh, who may have thrived on being held back, are victims of a system that is more concerned about the illusion of success presented by graduation rates than what is best for the individual child.

When parents, teachers, and special education experts all speak out on behalf of a child's best interests, it would behoove the leadership to listen to those who know the child best. Educational leaders who ignore the voices that have "opened their mouths . . . for the poor and needy" are essentially ignoring those who are a child's best advocate. When a system is built on a foundation of listening to these voices of advocacy, rather than obstinately imposing practices and procedures that fail to consider the individual children whom they affect, not only will those individual children flourish, but so, too, will the system as a whole.

WHEN THE SYSTEM FAILS TEACHERS

There are many ways the system fails kids, but unfortunately, they are not the only casualties of a broken system. Sometimes it is teachers, and even school communities, who fall victim to a system that is more concerned about the business bottom line than it is about the children and communities it is meant to serve. That was Mrs. C's story.

Mrs. C's school district recently decided to implement a teacher transfer policy that states teachers can be expected to move if they have been working in the same building for more than five years. Although such transfer policies have the potential to serve a purpose when implemented with compassion for the teacher's family situation, collaborative conversation, and a desire to do what is best for students, when blindly applied merely to satisfy an administrator's idea of an ambiguous quota, they have traumatic potential for the individuals affected.

Mrs. C's school district's administrative office is located in an urban center and serves many small rural communities within a hundred-mile radius. Working and living in a small town, she and her colleagues knew of this transfer policy, but her school had yet to be affected by it, presumably because it is often difficult enough to hire staff who want to commute to small rural schools, so why transfer *out* the local teachers who live there?

Mrs. C received a phone call during class one afternoon from her principal who asked if she had a couple of minutes to come down to the office. Curious, she told her class that she would be right back, never expecting for a moment that her life was about to be irrevocably changed.

"I am just going to rip the Band-Aid off," Mrs. C was told upon entering the office. "You are being transferred."

There is simply no way to describe Mrs. C's shock, because at first that was her only emotion. Her body started trembling uncontrollably. She started sweating. She could not believe that everything she had given to that school in the past nine years—her time, her energy, her dedication—was obviously of so little value, that she as an employee was of so little value, that she could be treated with such disregard.

When word got out in the community regarding Mrs. C's transfer, it erupted with rage towards the school district's callous treatment of one of their employees, with fury over the loss of a dedicated teacher, and with caring and support for their beloved educator.

No child could ever cause that much hurt in a teacher. And no child could ever cause such a tidal wave of emotion in an entire community. Only a faulty educational system has that much power.

Mrs. C was informed of her transfer on a Friday afternoon. By Monday, a committee had been formed of parents and community members who were planning meetings to figure out how to "Keep Mrs. C," a slogan that soon appeared on a billboard outside the school, on posters around town, and on social media. By Friday of that first week, the hallways were starting to smell of unwashed t-shirts worn daily by the beautiful children who had quickly made "Keep Mrs. C" clothes and paraphernalia to demonstrate their support.

After community meetings held at the local arena, the committee decided on a few actions they would undertake, including requesting a meeting with the school district CEO, the school board, and the creation of a petition. A letter campaign was also begun on Mrs. C's behalf and the district office, school board trustees, local politician's office, and Minister of Education were inundated with letters and pleas.

The community's chamber of commerce even got involved. They researched transfer policies in other school districts and put together a well-documented presentation regarding the benefits of employing local teachers in a small community school. They were given the opportunity to present their research and a petition that had been signed by over half of the entire community at a school board meeting. Meanwhile, the teachers' union was preparing to take the district to court and Mrs. C was learning more about the law and legal rights of employees and employers than she had ever wanted to know.

All of these efforts were to no avail.

Despite the community's raging outcry and students' devastated tears, the district remained firm that their decision was "better for the system." Mrs.

C was left dealing with weepy children in her classroom on an almost daily basis for the last couple of months of spring until school let out for the year.

This decision was not best for kids, not best for Mrs. C as a professional, nor was it best for the community affected by the transfer. When a decision hurts that many people, it cannot therefore be best for the system either.

The reality of this story is that Mrs. C's community did not win their fight. At the end of the day, she was still transferred and the students and parents who had cried with her since March were there to cry with her on the last day of school when she had to say goodbye.

What is hopefully apparent through the telling of this story, however, is that despite all that Mrs. C had lost in the district's enforced transfer, her community gave her something that no district or transfer policy could ever take away. Every single letter, signature on a petition, email, text message, visit, and every single "Keep Mrs. C" t-shirt made in one of the student's garages taught Mrs. C a lesson that the community was not even aware they were teaching.

In their efforts to keep Mrs. C in the building, she was made to feel valued, honored, and worth fighting for. As a result, the hard lesson to be learned from this story is that sometimes victory is not in winning the actual battle. Sometimes, the glory is in showing someone they were worth fighting for in the first place.

WORTH THE FIGHT

When you stand up for someone else, you give them a sense of value, honor, and worth so deep in their soul that regardless of the outcome of your fight, they know they were worth the battle. There is no greater feeling than the sense of worth you get when you realize someone values you enough to enter into a conflict on your behalf.

A veteran who served in the Canadian special forces has shared stories of his service with students in his community. While he can make them laugh with some of his stories about "jingle trucks" and killer Afghanistan spiders, they have also been moved to tears and heartbreak by some of his other stories that give them just a tiny snippet of insight into the horrendous conditions he has lived through, and continues to live with, in the aftermath of active duty. The students walk away from his presentation with nothing but utter and profound respect for the ingrained sense of loyalty and commitment to this country that propels people like him to sign up for service.

This veteran's first comment when he heard about this local teacher being transferred out of the community was "they ripped the banner off her back." Coming from someone who was willing to sign his life away for the sake of his country, he understood the sense of betrayal that Mrs. C was experiencing on a very different level.

Everything she had stood for, worked for, and sacrificed for, had been stripped away without so much as a "thank you for your commitment to this school," but rather, "I'm just going to rip the Band-Aid off." In ripping off that Band-Aid, the school district did exactly what this veteran so eloquently said, and also tore the banner off that she had so proudly attached to her back—a banner that reflected where she lived, her passion for integrating school and community, and her commitment to teaching students about service to that community. Just like that, it was gone.

But this veteran's other words of experience make it evident that this story does not have to end there. He has commented on how when he signed the paper that confirmed his service to his country, each and every other man or woman who signed that same paper instantaneously became his "brother," a person who had vowed that their life was expendable if it meant saving someone else's. This sense of brotherhood is inspiring; can you imagine working with colleagues who all share such a deep-rooted, unshakeable sense of trust in each other?

While the work teachers do in the classroom cannot possibly be compared to the sacrifices soldiers make in their service to their country, there is something to be learned from their understanding of "brotherhood." When soldiers sign their contracts to serve their country, they also sign up to fight on behalf of those who are unable or unwilling to fight for themselves.

As teachers, you will never be asked to put your lives on the line to defend others. You will not be asked to sacrifice months and years away from your families to protect the rights of others. You will not suffer the mind-altering consequences of witnessing violence and bloodshed, knowing first-hand the depravity of what humans are capable of inflicting on each other.

Teachers have none of those negative repercussions for signing a contract when they begin their profession, but they do have a similar obligation to fight for those children and colleagues who are unable or unwilling to fight for themselves. Those battles, when educators become the voice that speaks on behalf of others, are the ones that are most worth the fight. Not necessarily because you will win, but because you will have proven to those who need it most that someone believed enough in their value to speak on their behalf.

FIGHT WITH INTEGRITY

Often when people fight for something, they do it in the intensity of a moment without always looking around to see the impact that it might have on others. This single-minded focus can be positive in the exclusion of other distractions, but it also has the potential for negative repercussions. When you seek ways to right a wrong, either for yourself or for others, be cautious about any action you take in the event that it comes at the expense of justice for others.

In the passion of the moment, it is absolutely imperative that you pause, check your emotions, and ensure that your fight does not hurt others in the pursuit for the fairness and equality you seek for yourself. Because if you hurt others in your crusade, that dispels the integrity of what you are trying to do. And your goal, even if achieved, becomes tainted by that cost.

A particular advocate of Mrs. C's presented a good reminder of these truths when her community was fighting to keep her in their school. A retired teacher who had taught much of his career in the local school, had a passion for student leadership, and a commitment to community, volunteered to take a leadership role in trying to get Mrs. C's transfer reversed. While others commiserated with Mrs. C when she was transferred, this retired teacher also saw the negative long-term repercussions this transfer policy could have on the school and the community.

Also a concerned member of town council, this retired educator recognized that the involuntary transfer of local teachers out of the community meant that over the years, they might no longer have any local teachers working in their school who are invested in ensuring youth would receive quality educational and extra-curricular opportunities. Should the district continue to abide by their belief that every teacher must be moved within a five- to ten-year time span, that meant the entire local teaching staff would have to be relocated and replaced with commuting teachers who, while able to provide instruction, simply cannot facilitate a community-school connection when their own home community is a commute away.

With this concern sparking his motivation, this retired teacher became one of the most diligent members of the committee that had been formed on behalf of all local teachers and he was committed to seeing the fight through to the end in a positive way. While some well-meaning students and parents had all sorts of plans to show the school district's administration exactly what they thought of the transfer policy, this ex-teacher continued to be a calm voice of reason, encouraging people to fight with the integrity and respect for which the community was known.

He was often heard to say, "I still have hope," despite the many setbacks in his pursuit of justice. In the spirit of "practicing what we preach," this retired teacher showed through his actions that when you stand up for what you believe is right and do so with integrity and respect for everyone in the process, you may lose the battle, but you cannot, and will not, lose what matters most.

"OPEN YOUR MOUTHS FOR THE RIGHTS OF ALL"

Hopefully Josh's and Mrs. C's stories will resonate with you in ways that will inspire you to improve the school experiences of your students and colleagues. By putting into practice the verse upon which this chapter is based, consider vowing to "open your mouth for the rights of all." In other words, give others the gift of value and worthiness by speaking out for those who cannot speak for themselves and by fighting battles on behalf of those who cannot fight for themselves.

Rather than dwell on the cynicism towards illogical and hurtful policies that are an unfortunate reality of working within a flawed system, choose instead to focus on what you can control. Have faith in the power of voice and have hope in the power of action.

When Mrs. C's community "opened [their] mouths" for the rights of local teachers and for the best interests of their students, they gave her something that profoundly took the place of what her school district had taken away. Worth. Value. Honor. Those are the gifts that you have the power to bestow upon the children, colleagues, and community whom you serve whenever they need you to "open your mouth, judge righteously, [and] defend the rights of the poor and needy" (Proverbs 31: 9).

Chapter 11

Love Your Neighbor

"You shall love your neighbor as yourself."

Matthew 22:39

Teaching is more than a profession. When pursued with the passion of truly wanting to make a difference in the lives of those souls who fill your classroom, it becomes a life vocation. There is a significant difference between professionally teaching the content of a course and personally teaching the beautiful children who are taking the course. In fact, effective teachers understand that curriculum content is a good excuse to have kids in your classroom for the real lessons you can teach them about life, leadership, and service to others.

Service to others. In a society where students are constantly encouraged to think of themselves, to pursue whatever it is that will give them pleasure, to believe that they are entitled (there is that hateful word again!) to their own happiness even if it comes at a cost to other people, the concept of serving others is anathema to what seems to have become a global human right; that we should actually expect others to serve us.

Consider using your classroom to teach students that service is not what they should expect from the world, but rather what they should give. Develop your classroom into a space where curriculum outcomes are not only taught, but where these outcomes are strategically intertwined with activities that take students out of the building and into the community. It is of utmost importance that kids learn about what others in their community do for them, about the services their community provides that make it a great place to live, and how they can give back to the community in some small way.

There is also a bit of an ulterior motive underlying this desire to get students involved in the community. While you might see these children as a blessing in your life, as gifts with whom you get to spend your time alternately teaching and learning from, you are likely aware that not everyone sees teenagers in that light. "Kids these days" has been repeated so often that it is a mantra that probably makes your eyes roll in exasperation and frustration.

The truth is, "kids these days" are incredible people. They have talents and skills with technology no one could have ever predicted that will help them find future success in a world where tech is inevitable. They have global networks and experiences through traveling and internet connections that have the power to shape the world into a global village in unprecedented ways. They are inundated with massive amounts of information every minute, and every second of every day as their phones "bing" with incoming messages, news article headlines popping up on their screens, and advertisements, all through which they must learn to focus when their attention is drawn in a million different directions.

"Kids these days" are growing up and learning differently than any generation before them. Educators and parents need to embrace the potential that has for society by teaching them to serve the people in it. And unless kids are given the opportunities to serve others, they will continue to remain wrapped up in their own little worlds of isolation, texting the friend who is sitting beside them, rather than developing the simple skills of communication that will help them make the world a better place.

What follows in this chapter are a few examples and stories of how educators have found ways to get their students out in the community or how they have invited the community in to be a part of their students' learning experiences. This chapter is certainly not intended as an exhaustive checklist of things you should do, nor can it even be presumed that these exact same ideas will work in your community. Rather, these ideas are meant to spark your own and the lessons learned from each experience are intended to help you identify the possibilities for similar community connections.

TEA WITH SENIORS

A language arts curriculum for fifteen-year-old students provides the following thematic questions as a lens through which they are asked to study literature and compose written assignments:

- How are the issues that children face today different from the issues experienced by children in previous generations?
- How and why have the roles of children and youth changed over the years?

Ms. R recognized these prescribed curriculum thematic questions for what they were—a rich opportunity to engage her students with the senior citizens in the community. Deciding these questions could be the basis for conversation, she set about planning "tea time" with the local seniors' club, and in doing so, provided a hands-on learning experience that literally had her students serving others, and became a much-anticipated annual community event.

To begin facilitating this event each year, Ms. R has students write a note to the local seniors' club, inviting them to tea during one of their class periods. In preparation for the big day, the students ask the cooking class to bake dainties and prepare tea (also a great authentic experience for the cooking class) and set up and decorate tables in an available room in the school. As a class, the students brainstorm conversation starters and ideas for discussion to alleviate the nerves of having to entertain the seniors as most of their experiences with the elderly are limited to visits with Grandma and Grandpa.

When the day arrives, Ms. R's pride in her students is evident. Even the "edgy" kids whose troubled lives cause habitual scowls and negative attitudes bring their best to this event. Dressed in semi-formal clothes, and having ditched the ball caps in favor of styling their hair, students take it seriously when Ms. R tells them that this is an exciting event for these seniors and they will be coming dressed in their best so please do not insult them by showing up in filthy, tattered work clothes.

The designated "greeters" nervously smile and meet the seniors at the front door of the school, proudly offering their arms to escort them to the tearoom where the rest of the class awaits them. The next hour becomes one where memories are created; the senior guests are thrilled and touched by the obvious effort that goes into preparing the room for their visit but even more so by having these attentive young adults serve them and show a genuine interest in the stories they have to tell.

If you attempt a similar event, ensure there are a few decks of cards available and it will amuse you how horrified the seniors are to discover most of these kids have no idea how to play cards in general, and rummy in particular. Then sit back and watch as the seniors start shuffling and dealing with proficiency born of years of practice and delight in the opportunity to teach their captive audience the ins and outs of their favorite games.

When the time is up, students and seniors alike are disappointed and an event that typically begins with an uncertain class of teenagers timidly welcoming a few elderly people into their school because their teacher said this was part of their language arts course, culminates in a group of people chatting and laughing their way down the hallway, reluctant to say goodbye to a new and unexpected friendship.

As Ms. R's students head off to their next classes, the rest of the student body and staff take notice of their dress, their positive and joyful demeanor, and listen as the kids excitedly share their stories. The senior students grin as they listen, remembering when they had had the experience during their time in Ms. R's class and the younger students smile skeptically, not really understanding how tea with "old people" could possibly be that much fun.

As fantastic as tea time with the seniors was for Ms. R's students, this tradition became merely the beginning of something bigger, something that had lasting and valuable implications for the school community as a whole. The initial relationships forged over tea and cards continues to develop when this language arts class annually accepts the senior club's reciprocated invitation to attend one of their "Old Time Dances" with live fiddle music and more two-stepping, polkaing, and square dancing than the kids have ever seen.

Completely forced out of their comfort zone, the kids blush with embarrassment when a lovely elderly lady or gentleman approaches with their hand outstretched, asking them to dance. Unable to say no, they are led onto the dance floor where they nervously and gingerly try to follow their partner's lead around the dance floor, trying (sometimes successfully) not to step on anyone's toes or lose their balance in their uncoordinated efforts to learn the intricate steps of old-time dancing. On the walk back to the school afterwards, the wholesome laughter and genuine joy over the experience cannot be contained.

Community. That is the "something bigger" that this story is really about. The memories and laughter alone made the experience worth Ms. R's effort of planning it, but these kinds of "lessons" go deeper than just reflecting on stories. Rather than seeing these same children as the "kids these days" who are skateboarding on the sidewalks, driving down the streets blaring their music too loudly, or rudely pushing past them in the grocery store, the seniors in this community now see them as the children who served them tea and giggled self-consciously as they awkwardly attempted to learn the dance steps that were second nature to their senior partners.

And rather than see the seniors as slow and bothersome people who do not get out of the way on the sidewalks, drive annoyingly slow down Main Street, and block the store aisles with their carts and busybody chitchat, the teenagers in this community now see them as keepers of wisdom, entertaining and humorous storytellers, and worthy of their utmost respect for the lives they have led and the harsh realities they have faced.

In short, experiences like "tea time" with the seniors help both students and community members to see each other as neighbors and to begin to fulfill the wisdom of the verse on which this chapter is based; to "love your neighbor."

The questions from the language arts curriculum that inspired these events were answered in Ms. R's class in ways that no amount of reading literature, viewing documentaries, or researching history could ever begin to touch. *How are the issues that children face today different from the issues experienced by children in previous generations? How and why have the roles of children and youth changed over the years?* Just ask the students and seniors in your community after they have had the chance to connect through tea and dancing. They will tell you.

CONNECTING COMMUNITY AND CURRICULUM

The seniors' tea and dancing are just a couple of examples of how you might intertwine community, curriculum, and kids. Other teachers' examples of community engagement include a math treasure hunt that was created to have students map and graph their way around town, going to local businesses to get their next clues. Business owners text selfie pictures with students when they arrive, glad to welcome kids into their shops for those moments of fun and authentic learning.

Another curriculum-community connection includes the social studies teacher who invited community members into the school to watch and judge as the senior class presented their debates on a global issue, an event that had become a rite of passage in that school. The teacher commented that she will never forget the horror on one student's face when he approached her after the debate and said, "I seriously cannot believe I just debated the negative side of religion in front of a pastor!" He did such a brilliant job of his presentation, however, that his team won, despite some potential bias on the part of one particular judge!

When a leadership class was learning about meeting protocols and structures, city council was happy to get involved. Not only were they willing to answer students' questions about local governance, but they also offered an authentic experience by allowing the class to use their boardroom for a mock townhall meeting. Sitting around the table where community decisions were made while students practiced their own meeting protocol was an engaging lesson in governance.

Another valuable instance of community involvement could be described in the profound respect encapsulated by one student's response following a local military veteran's talk with grade twelve students about service, loyalty, and post-traumatic stress. "Mrs. P, in all the years of listening to guest speakers or Ted Talks on the internet in class, that was seriously the best presentation I have ever heard." Not only did the class learn from this veteran about military service, but they learned the story behind the courageous man who fought for his country and still fights the effects of those battles every day with the memories that haunt him.

The examples are endless. There are many incredible opportunities to enlist the help of your community as you work to educate the kids in your classroom. Do not go this journey alone and do not be afraid to ask for help.

Ultimately, bringing the curriculum into the community, or vice versa, is about relationships. Finding those opportunities to connect the curriculum to your community not only enhances your relationship with the people whose school you are serving, but it also fosters relationships between the kids and the people with whom they share these common roots. Providing these types of opportunities for your students does more than educate them about curriculum standards; it teaches them about people and about community.

If your students are like most teenagers, many of them cannot wait to escape high school, get out of town, and take on the big world. While kids should be encouraged to seek adventures and explore what life has to offer, consider making it a personal mission to help kids see their time in their community as a place they will be proud to call home—a place where they would want to return, if only for a visit. Kids should not view their place of childhood as a place from which they need to escape, but rather a place they remember with fondness and appreciation. Simply attending school in a building within a city or a town cannot possibly nurture these kinds of feelings. Only relationships with the people who live there can do that.

SERVICE THAT GOES BEYOND CURRICULUM

Building relationships between community members and students can begin by exploring curriculum connections that enrich the lessons you intend for your students to learn, but what will develop these relationships on a deeper level that will help achieve this personal mission of getting kids to be proud of their community is teaching kids about voluntary service.

Service is the first and most important role of any educator. Teachers should feel obligated to serve the children in their classroom and the parents who have entrusted them with their precious kids. Teachers should also feel obligated to serve the community whose future rests on the success and education of the future leaders who are walking the halls of the school.

You might vehemently disagree with this perspective and question why teachers should feel obligated to serve. Rather than teachers serving the kids, parents, and community, should it not be the other way around? After all, teachers are paid to teach. Kids, parents, and community members should be grateful for the education you provide, right?

Yet if teachers expect to be served, and model that expectation, then who will ever be led to serve? Students mimic what they see. And when their classroom role models practice the service that they preach, then they too will be more likely to view helping others and volunteering in their community as worthwhile and valuable endeavors. And when they see your joy in service, they will come to recognize that it is not something to which they are entitled, but rather something that can bring them joy in the giving.

This belief is quite likely not something you learned in university when you were learning how to teach. You have also likely never heard it at a professional development seminar for teachers. But maybe service should be part of the teacher training program and part of professional development expectations. Not only should service be a crucial part of teacher education, but it also has a place in curriculum content. Some of the most valuable lessons that can be taught occur when teachers work with kids on projects outside of the classroom, projects that have little to do with teaching them the curriculum and everything to do with them learning about life.

When you step out of the classroom and work with students in the role of a coach, advisor, or mentor in another capacity, you will have unique opportunities to push kids out of their comfort zones and they will likely push you out of yours. You will get the pleasure of watching students grow and develop into compassionate young adults with a mature understanding of teamwork when they strive to achieve a common goal.

Provide your kids with a chance to serve others and you will be amazed at how much more they beg you to let them give. "Kids these days" have a capacity for compassion and service that we do not expect nor ask of them often enough. Let them surprise you.

STUDENT LEADERSHIP SERVICE IDEAS

Most schools have student leadership councils of some sort. These students are busy, active leaders who try to elevate the spirit in their buildings and provide their peers with events and activities that make their time in school more memorable.

What follows are examples taken from the yearly schedule of one school's student leadership council. Note that, like the community-classroom examples from before, this is nowhere near an exhaustive list, nor should it be considered a checklist of things that should be done in a school. Your student leadership council likely does things very differently and is equally as effective. These are mere ideas that could possibly spark your own list and they are also intended to give you a moment's pause to reflect on how much your students may already be doing.

If the students in your building are already engaged in these types of leadership activities, then consider this a challenge to you to support their work, help them, and appreciate them, regardless of whether you are the teacher advisor for your school's student leadership council. Your engagement in their work means the world to these kids.

Often, an effective student leadership council's school year begins with a fall retreat about two weeks prior to school opening. Teacher advisors take the students out on a day of adventure and team-building activities where they reminisce about the last school year, tell stories about their summer, make plans for the upcoming year, and begin building the relationships that will sustain them as a team throughout the year. While other kids are soaking up the last days of summer, these kids' service has already begun.

September is always a busy month with school startup. As most other schools in Canada do, the student leadership council hosts a Terry Fox Run to raise money for cancer research. They celebrate this national hero not just by recognizing his commitment to a worthy cause with the traditional walk around the community, but by using this as the first opportunity to welcome the community into the school. The council hosts a community BBQ and invites the elementary students to join the high school, pairing up grades so that the high school kids get the opportunity to serve the younger ones, even if they are not part of the planning committee.

This Terry Fox annual event is in addition to the multiple football BBQs the student council hosts at every home game in the fall where the kids work shifts, volunteering their time to make each game more of a crowd-pleasing event. When October rolls around, these student volunteers will often continue their football BBQs and add in an old-fashioned Quarter Carnival to their schedule to celebrate Halloween. Traditionally held the evening before Halloween, the high school is flooded with children and adults dressed in their costumes as they enjoy simple carnival games and activities.

As October fades into November, the student leadership council works with the staff to plan a Remembrance Day service for the school that honors the sacrifices that were made to guarantee the freedoms we all enjoy. The council also hosts a "Movember" fundraiser with a moustache-growing competition among the male staff and students whose proceeds go to cancer research.

Amidst the chaos of the Christmas season and the multitude of school-based activities, the council also generates and collects food items from the student body to donate to the local food bank to make Christmas a little less stressful for some families. Loose change is also collected and used to purchase gifts for families across the globe through a variety of charitable organizations.

When the new year begins, the SLC works in tandem with the recreation board in the community to plan and host "Hockey Day" activities, including an annual staff versus student hockey game. February sees the student council raising money for a provincial fundraiser whose proceeds go to helping families with children who have special needs. In March, these same kids are fundraising again, this time by planning and executing their annual wake-a-thon with the thousands of dollars raised going to an organization of their choice in their own community.

April's Easter and Anti-Bullying "Pink Day" campaign are celebrated with a full morning of activities and pancake breakfast for the elementary students. As the ice hockey season winds down and the snow melts, a community street hockey tournament fundraiser for STARS Air Ambulance is hosted.

You might think that by the time May rolls around, this group of busy kids has had enough and is prepared to relax and start thinking about summer, but instead they quickly check off the last remaining details from their events in April and get busy planning a community Canadian Cancer Relay for Life event to coincide with similar events held across Canada at the end of the month.

They culminate their school year with an annual "Summer Fest" in June that changes in details every year, but traditionally features a BBQ, a lot of water on a strategically chosen hot day, and a mud pit. There were a lot of naysayers and hesitation when this particular activity was introduced, but the students found ways around all the obstacles (including an outdoor shower courtesy of the volunteer firefighters) and the wacky idea became a much-anticipated annual event.

These kids are like the Energizer Bunny—they just do not quit. You may be concerned about burnout—both yours and the kids.' The truth is you will find these kids *want* to be together, working towards a common goal. They feed off each other's energy and ideas and every year, the annual events you plan get better. Not only do the events get better, but the community's support over the years will grow in a way that reflects the value they see in the work the kids do to host these events.

IT TAKES A VILLAGE

Doug Griffiths, author of *13 Ways to Kill Your Community,* theorizes that the biggest challenge communities face in building a sense of unity is that "our wealth has made us complacent and we have not had to work together to build as we have in the past. We are independent people who do not need a community for the same reason, namely for survival, as we did in the past, and so we have lost our sense of how to hold our community together" (Griffiths 2011, 156).

The seniors' tea stories that they share with students about how neighbors used to work together to raise barns, crops, and children are testament to Griffiths' belief that, in the old days, survival led to a necessary building of community. That does not mean, however, that this generation is without hope. While today's youth may not grow up to share inspiring stories of hard physical labor and relying on neighbors to help them survive, they can still be given opportunities to grow up with other stories of community.

There are stories of business owners donating funds to the football team to show their appreciation of the players who went and laid sod at the newly built daycare. Or stories of a group of teenage students, heartbroken and grieving over the Humboldt Broncos 2018 crash that claimed the lives of 16 team members, planning a community street hockey tournament and BBQ to honor the victims by raising money for STARS Air Ambulance. And maybe it is simple stories like when the high school kids host the annual Quarter Carnival with pride, knowing they have carried on the tradition that began long before their time that they remember enjoying as young children.

Small things or huge events, each and every one of these stories contributes to the sense of community.

In a book about teaching and education, you may wonder why a long and detailed chapter on community has been included. Although the people of this generation may have become an "independent people who do not need community" (Griffiths 2011, 156), perhaps the opposite is true. Perhaps this simply means we need community now more than we ever have before.

In a world where people's independence is second nature and their ability to connect globally leaves them disconnected locally, it takes a concerted effort to build the sense of togetherness that used to be a by-product of survival. If educators and parents do not make that concerted effort with this generation of youth who are about to become the future leaders of these places we call home, those stories of community will dissolve from fond remembrances into myths.

Although people may no longer need each other to survive, we still depend on each other to thrive. And while we may no longer need our neighbors to help us build a barn, we do still need each other to build people. The old truth that "it takes a village to raise a child" will never change. It is our responsibility to ensure that village stays intact, and, even more importantly, to teach our children to value and serve that same village.

Chapter 12

When We Stumble

"For we all stumble in many ways."

James 3:2

This is a humbling chapter to include, but if a book entitled *Practice What You Preach* contains a chapter about a flawed education system and another chapter on the importance of kids learning from their mistakes, then what other choice is there but to turn that mirror around and reflect on the lessons teachers can learn from their own flaws?

These lessons come at the cost of pride when you admit you messed up, but it is a very small price to pay for the opportunity those mistakes will give you to learn, grow, and get better as a teacher. Not only does humbling yourself help you get better as a professional, acknowledging your own faults will establish an environment of trust and respect where students can also make mistakes from which they can learn, grow, and get better as people.

There are easily enough stories of classroom trials and tribulations to write an entire book on this topic, let alone a mere chapter devoted to it. Yet as humbling, and sometimes embarrassing, as they are, these stories need to be told. When teachers do not model how to admit to their own challenges in the classroom, share their frustrations in overcoming difficulties, and explain their regret over mistakes they wish they could undo, then students in the classroom and colleagues in the staffroom are often left feeling like they are the only ones making mistakes.

Nothing could be further from the truth. Every teacher encounters challenges. Every teacher experiences frustration. And every educator has regrets. The power in those challenges, frustrations and regrets is the opportunity they provide educators to learn from each other, a power that fails to reach its potential when teachers are more prone to hiding their failures than sharing them.

What follows is one such story of challenge, frustration, and regret. It is only one story among millions that occur daily in any given classroom. But it is one in which teachers may see themselves and see their students. And hopefully it is one from which you can learn along with the teacher who was also humbled; and then learned.

LEARNING THROUGH STORY

Picture for a moment the stereotypical class clown, the child who makes the day brighter with his or her goofiness and who can be counted on to provide laughter even in the untimeliest of situations. The child who, when you ask to "hush," you do so with a smile lurking at the corner of your lips because, despite needing him to let the rest of the class focus, you cannot help but anticipate his next moment of levity.

That student was Grant. Grant was in grade 12 when Mrs. M really had the chance to work with him and get to know him and by that time his reputation as the class goofball was well established. Not only did he provide the class with endless fodder for humor, but by this point, he had also become the subject of many jokes—his own as well as others'.

Looking back now, it makes Mrs. M cringe to remember how often Grant would joke at his own expense and the entire class would all laugh with him. It makes her shudder to think of the regularity with which his peers would also make jokes at his expense, and everyone would all laugh with him. The class laughed *with* him so often that they failed to realize when he had stopped laughing and they were now just laughing *at* him.

Mrs. M says she will never forget the moment in English class where class clown Grant was reading aloud and mispronounced a word. As any teacher would, her normal reaction would have been to jump down any child's throat who had the nerve to laugh at a peer's mispronunciation of a word. But since mispronunciation had been one of Grant's typical tactics to get everyone to laugh, Mrs. M responded in an untypical teacher fashion, and laughed along with the students when "militia" came out as "mil—it—ee—ah."

Years later, Mrs. M relates that she can still see Grant's face turn red as his embarrassment, anger, and humiliation collided into an unprecedented surge of emotions that had nothing to do with laughter and everything to do with hurt.

"So I said something wrong," he yelled. "So WHAT?! All you guys ever do is make fun of me. I am sick of it. I am so sick of being the joke in this class."

And then he turned to Mrs. M, looked her in the eyes, and said, "And you are the worst. You are the *TEACHER*."

Grant threw down his book and left the room. He did not storm out, as would have seemingly befit his raging emotions. That would have almost been easier to take. Instead, he left utterly dejected. Head down, shoulders bent, this child; this six-foot, gruff, football-playing young man, walked out of that classroom, hurt. Because of the actions of the students, yes. But worse, because of the actions of his teacher.

The class was quiet except for a couple of whispers and nervous giggles as kids tried to figure out if Grant was going to come back into the room and make them laugh with a "Gotcha!" exclamation—a more common and expected finale to his unusual display of drama. But Mrs. M knew better. She knew those emotions were raw, deep, and real. And she knew that this was no joke.

Telling the rest of the class to keep reading, Mrs. M followed Grant out of the room, down the hallway, and into the weight room where he had spent many hours over the past two years working to build his strength for the football field, a room where his physical strength was currently no match for the power of his emotions.

As she walked into the room, which was thankfully devoid of any other students, she saw a kid whose joking good nature had been obliterated by insult and whose easy laugh had been devastated by betrayal. Mrs. M saw those emotions and more in the stooped shoulders as he sat on a weight bench, hands rubbing his face, trying to stave off the tears. Her heart, which had cracked the second he walked out of her classroom, shattered completely. She was responsible for this. She, who had professed to live by the belief that every child needs to be loved and respected, was now faced with the reality that she had failed this child miserably by not giving him the love and respect at a time when he needed it most.

Mrs. M and Grant talked for a long time, Grant rarely taking his face out of his hands to look her in the eye. Accustomed to a jovial kid who never lacked the confidence for eye contact, this avoidance of a personal connection spoke volumes about both the depth of his hurt and his anger toward Mrs. M for her part in causing it. As they spoke, she learned a great deal about Grant that she had never sought to find out before, having always taken his class clown persona for granted.

Apparently Grant's application to college, where he had hoped to play football, had recently been rejected. His parents' agriculture business was struggling and the financial stress in his house was causing a rift in a previously stable home life. Grant's older brother had just returned home from university after having dropped out due to serious mental-health issues. Life had just dealt Grant too many hard blows in a short amount of time and those details, combined with being the subject of an entire classroom's laughter, had simply pushed him past the breaking point.

Mrs. M listened. She cared. And she apologized. Profusely and sincerely.

Mrs. M wishes she could say that they shook hands and parted as friends. She would love to be able to tell this story by saying it ended with Grant regaining respect for her and that they went back to class with a firm foundation re-established that was based on understanding and compassion.

But that would be a lie and it would be a disservice to the depth of the hurt Grant felt. A mere apology could not undo the betrayal he had felt when a classroom of kids laughed at his mistake, and rather than stop them from causing embarrassment and shame, his teacher contributed to it by joining in.

A case could be made to defend Mrs. M's actions by explaining how Grant had done similar things in class before for the sake of getting a laugh, but the truth is, had she been in tune with what Grant was going through, she would have recognized the situation for what it was. And she did not. Mrs. M failed to see the signs that should have been telltale for days, maybe even weeks, prior to that incident, that Grant was not himself and that the class clown was no longer performing. Had Mrs. M been more aware and more cognizant of what he was going through, she would never have made such a drastic and hurtful mistake.

But she did. And no apology could erase that moment. As Mrs. M and Grant left the weight room, he trudged ahead of her, choosing to distance himself from her rather than walk beside her. That physical distance left Mrs. M with a lot to process.

When you love your job because you love your kids, there is nothing worse than knowing they are breaking inside and you cannot fix it. Nothing worse, that is, except the humbling and devastating knowledge that you are part of the reason they are broken.

When Grant came back to class the next day, Mrs. M chose not to address the outburst but chose instead to continue on with "business as normal," feeling that the last thing Grant needed was any more attention brought to the incident and the emotions that had caused it. She was very careful, however, to lay the groundwork that day for reinforcing the rules of respect that had always been her mantra, but which she had failed to apply to Grant the previous day. When another student teased him about something unrelated to English class, she quickly interrupted and gently reminded his friend to get back to work.

Mrs. M knew the road ahead would be challenging as, like her, his peers were only ever accustomed to Grant wanting to joke and be the joke himself. They did not have the background information that she had learned yesterday to help put his more sullen and quiet disposition into context. It took a long time of consistent reminders and her own demonstrations of respect to break kids of the habit of teasing Grant. And in the process, it dawned on her how often he had become the brunt of jokes. The class was simply so used to laughing with Grant that they, Mrs. M included, had become completely oblivious to how often they were laughing at him.

Mrs. M found it very difficult to achieve the balance she was seeking between ensuring students treated Grant with respect without drawing more attention to him and disclosing his confidence that he no longer wanted to be the class clown. By the end of the term, Mrs. M believes her persistence paid off when Grant was comfortable enough to make small jokes (in which he was never the target) and smile when others laughed. But she admits that she never felt a connection between them rebuild. She knew he appreciated her efforts and respected her for them, but the day she laughed at him when she should have defended him was the day she shattered the opportunity she had to gain this student's trust.

Mrs. M still feels shame when she reflects on Grant's story. She is sick that she allowed the incident to happen, but, worse, she is horrified that the conditions in her classroom had escalated to the point where that incident was almost inevitable. How could she not have seen that Grant was increasingly becoming the brunt of the jokes rather than the creator of the jokes? How could she have missed the fact that Grant's confidence was unraveling due to the uncontrollable factors going wrong in his life? How could she have missed that the smiling, laughing child was no longer?

LEARNING FROM THE HURT

The troubling thing about this story is the concern that a teacher's obliviousness to one child's hurt might also be hurting other kids in similar ways. The unfortunate truth is that this is very likely the case. Despite your best intentions, teachers simply cannot know the private details of every kid's life well enough to be attuned to the emotions they bring to the classroom each day. You are guaranteed to miss the sensitive and vulnerable state in which some students are enveloped as they sit in their desks, both because they are very good at hiding emotions they do not want others to see, and because you are often focused on, and distracted by, the many other needs in the classroom.

Mrs. M had to come to terms with the fact that she probably could not have ever known Grant's true state of mind, but the lesson from her story is that his sense of betrayal could have been prevented by staying true to the rules of every student's entitlement to respect. Grant deserved Mrs. M's respect by virtue of the fact that he was a student in her classroom. End of story.

Mrs. M messed up that day. Horribly and sickeningly messed up. But the experience has the power to showcase a lesson that, hopefully, may help others become better teachers and better people. Teachers have to learn to accept their own limitations in the sense that they cannot possibly know the intimate details of every child's story and be a therapist and counselor for each hurting child. But they can absolutely ensure that their classroom is a place of love and respect for each individual who walks through that door. And if each child's sense of welcome is genuine and heartfelt, then they will soon trust you enough to share their stories.

Because of stories like Grant's, you can never assume you have earned that sense of trust. Earning students' trust requires a tireless commitment of diligent adherence to standards of respect that have to be explicitly taught and implicitly expected in every interaction. And despite the hard work that goes into building this trust, it can be broken with one misplaced joke or laugh. When described that way, this journey of building trust in a classroom hardly seems worth the effort, but there is nothing worth more than when kids are honest with you and share their stories with you. Because then, not only can you help reach them where they are with the curriculum content you are responsible for teaching them, but you can reach them where they are as human beings. And help them grow.

This is not a responsibility to take lightly, but it is ever an honor to be blessed to carry such a welcome burden.

Chapter 13

Faith, Hope, and Love

> *"And now these three remain: faith, hope and love. But the greatest of these is love."*
>
> 1st Corinthians 13:13

This ancient, familiar, and oft-used-at weddings Bible verse may seem a bit out of context in a book about education. Yet when considered through the lens of "practicing what you preach," what more could teachers possibly need in the classroom other than the three values that are listed in this verse? Faith, hope, and love. Not only are these three principles valuable enough to be preached, but success in a classroom depends upon them being put into practice. When faith, hope, and love are the basis of a teacher's interactions with students, and the teacher is intentionally diligent about putting each of them into practice, every student in the classroom benefits.

FAITH

Although each chapter has been built around a verse from the Christian Bible, this book itself is not a presentation of religious beliefs. The verses were intended only as an exploration of possible practices teachers can put into place that will enrich their own classroom experience, and even more importantly, the classroom experience of their students.

These possible practices, although individually based on a specific biblical phrase, have even more significance when considered from a faith-based foundation upon which a classroom philosophy can be built. A classroom built on the faith that each person was perfectly created for a purpose and has a reason for being will inevitably also be a classroom that welcomes each student with acceptance for their individuality.

Regardless of your religious background, the students walking into your classroom deserve to be greeted by a teacher who lives out the belief that each one of them was unerringly created for a very specific purpose. These children deserve to be taught by someone who appreciates their uniqueness, beauty, and potential. And they deserve to be mentored by someone who has faith that you are in their classroom, and they are in yours, for a reason that has been determined by One whose wisdom far exceeds that of any human's.

When teachers live out this belief that, despite trials and tribulations, they were brought together with their students for a reason, students' behavior, actions, and achievements will ultimately reflect that persistent faith.

The reason and the purpose of a teacher's interactions with a child will not always be clear. Sometimes they are apparent early in the teacher-student relationship, like when the student and teacher "click" on the first day of class and a rapport is quickly established that lasts the entirety of their school career and develops into a valued adult friendship in the future. Sometimes the reason and purpose are not evident until, for example, a teacher receives a letter from a graduating student that brings her to tears because, in the student's silent and unassuming way, she had no idea of the depth to which she had reached that child's soul.

Sometimes the reason and the purpose for a teacher–student classroom experience are never revealed, and that is when it is the most difficult to have faith that they exist. Yet ancient wisdom reminds us that is the very essence of faith—"the assurance of things hoped for and the conviction of things unseen" (Hebrews 11:1). Teachers have the option to choose, time and again, to believe in that assurance and conviction because it means that teaching is not just a job to work at until retirement.

Rather, teaching is a calling that you are intended to answer until it has been fulfilled.

HOPE

"Hope is the only thing stronger than fear."

Although this quote does not come from one of the greatest books ever written (like the Bible) or a literary classic (like *To Kill A Mockingbird*), but rather from a popular dystopian series, *The Hunger Games*, it has significant meaning for this chapter. The antagonist of the story, President Snow, commented that "hope is the only thing stronger than fear" in reference to the people who were rebelling against his dictatorship. His intent was to squash the hope they had found in the defiant actions of the protagonist. He knew that if they continued to hope for change, hope for peace, and hope for a different way of life, he would lose the control he had over them, the control he had gained through the fear he had imposed with his harsh dictatorship. And he was not about to let that happen.

Students are living in a time where fear has a different flavor than past generations. They have not experienced war, famine, or depression. Their fearful experiences, however, are no less real, especially for the adults responsible for these children: the easy availability of drugs, the manipulation of children's beliefs by ever-present media, the inescapable lure of social media with its constant buzzing and notifications, and their readiness for life after high school. These are just some of the fears that parents and educators may have for children of this generation.

Youth, on the other hand, have all sorts of fears of their own: the overwhelming peer pressure to fit in, facing the consequences of poor decisions, making a sports team or drama cast, and getting into college. The list could go on—possibly endlessly. And each and every one of these fears is valid, real, and for some, debilitating.

That is where the reassurance of this seemingly innocuous quote comes to mind. What is stronger than these fears—these fears that are valid, real, and debilitating?

Hope.

Can it be that simple? How is hope possibly stronger than fearing the worst in any of those above situations?

But then, how can it *not* be?

Hope is like the pussy willows found along the roadside on a -30°C spring morning. Their existence, every year, is simple evidence of hope. Defying all logic that anything can possibly sprout, grow, and thrive in the midst of frigid conditions, pussy willows decorate the roadside every year as evidence that the frigidity of winter cannot last forever. And that something better, warmer, and more conducive to life is yet to come.

That is the hope kids need. In the midst of the frigid conditions of living in fear, and during circumstances when being hopeful defies all logic, students need to be taught to persevere with the stubborn optimism of the pussy willow that survives a -30°C morning because it *knows* and *believes* that spring is coming. Maya Angelou sees the battle between fear and hope as a choice that everyone has the power to make: "hope and fear cannot occupy the same space. Invite one to stay."

Teachers must model what that invitation looks like. Rather than fear that they will make the wrong choices, show students that you hope they will make the right ones. Rather than fear the powerful lure of technology and social media, use it to demonstrate the hope you have that it will make them better global citizens with an unprecedented opportunity to connect the world and make it a better place.

When kids witness you actively inviting hope to take the place of your fears, you will inadvertently teach them to do the same. Rather than being afraid they will not fit it, kids can learn to hope that they can find ways to include others. Rather than fear the consequences of a mistake they made, they can learn to hope that they can find a way to rectify their error, seek forgiveness, and learn from the experience. Rather than fear what the future holds for them, kids can learn to view the unknown with anticipation and hope.

Above all, do not teach kids to hope merely for the sake of believing in an ambiguous concept. Teach students to have hope for the future because through their actions they have the power to ensure that their hopes become reality. Like Maya Angelou's invitation to hope, you would not invite guests to your house and then leave the minute they walk through the door. If you teach students to invite hope to replace their fears, they need to learn to actively treat it like an honored guest in their homes by consciously making an effort to feed that hope and ensure that it continues to thrive.

... AND LOVE. BUT THE GREATEST OF THESE IS LOVE.

Among the millions of other memories that you will leave your students from the time they spent in your classroom, do they know this about you? Do they know that you love your job? And most importantly, *do they know you love your job because you love them?*

There is not a single child who will walk through your classroom doors who does not need, and is not worthy of, love. There is no question that some of them are not easy to love; in fact, some of them make it almost impossible. But hang onto the faith that people are not created by accident, that each person has a purpose and that everyone's reason for being is equally as important as the next.

A simplistic way of illustrating each person's value can be found on an elementary baseball team. Coaches must constantly repeat the mantra that all nine positions on the field and the few cheerleader positions on the bench are of equal importance. For young players who only want to pitch or play shortstop, however, this is a difficult concept. They recognize that the pitcher and catcher may touch the ball a hundred times more than any other player, and that the shortstop typically makes the flashiest plays, and instantly covet one of those high-profile positions. Yet each member contributes something of value that would make the team less if they were not a part of it.

The classroom, the community, the country, and the world, all abide in the same way as a baseball team in the sense that each one would be less as a whole if only one person is lost. Sixteenth-century poet John Donne expressed this same sentiment with eloquence:

> No man is an island entire of itself;
> every man is a piece of the continent, a part of the main;
> if a clod be washed away by the sea,
> Europe is the less . . . (Donne n.d.)

Every child who takes up space in your classrooms must also take up space in your heart. Each one of them must feel they are of equal importance and that your classroom would be less if they were not present. Likely several faces come to mind when you think about how much *easier* a classroom might be to manage if they were not in it; but teachers do not get into this profession believing it would be easy. You got into teaching because you believed that every student matters, is valuable, and that you can help make a difference in their lives. And when they walk through your classroom door, they should *know* their teacher believes this to be true.

LOVE: FROM 1ST CORINTHIANS TO THE CLASSROOM

Examining the rest of the descriptions of love from 1st Corinthians 13, not as one might normally do in the context of a wedding ceremony, but in the context of the classroom, provides an even deeper understanding of an educator's true purpose.

1. "Love is patient, love is kind."

Although this verse is likely self-explanatory, there is no doubt that sometimes it can be the most challenging. Loving the students in a classroom means having patience with them and understanding that often their not-so-lovable behavior stems from a situation beyond their control. Focusing on the joy students can bring rather than the hurt they cause is covered in chapter 6, so it does not need to be dwelled on again here, other than to include a gentle reminder.

Children who are hurting will often hurt others, including you. They will lash out in defensive anger, hurting anyone in the vicinity of their wrath. Know and have compassion for the truth that the pain they are inflicting is a reflection of the pain they are experiencing. Be patient with their behavior, be kind in your interactions with them, but above all, love the being that was put in your classroom and in your life, and have faith that they are there for a very necessary reason.

2. "It does not envy, it does not boast, it is not proud."

You might stumble over this verse in your humility and inability to see the greatness you have to offer your students and your colleagues. You may feel that although you have learned a great deal in your years as an educator, it may not be of any use or significance to anyone else. And you may even be concerned that if you presume to have some sort of "wisdom" to share, that it is boasting and prideful to assume others would want you to share that knowledge.

Angela Maiers in Todd Nesloney's book *Kids Deserve It!* encourages teachers to believe in themselves and the gifts they can contribute, both to the classroom when these gifts are shared with students, and to the larger world of education when they are shared with colleagues. "'When you are an educator, you have brilliant ideas. And when you are not sharing your brilliant ideas, you are doing a disservice to others in the field who could and want to learn from you'" (Nesloney and Welcome 2016).

Teachers must be willing to share and learn from each other, without any envy for a colleague's success and without boasting or taking pride in their own. Sharing the wisdom you have gained from experience is not boasting, rather it is a demonstration of love for the profession, and love for the children whom you may never teach, but others will, children who deserve the best that you have to offer.

3. "It does not dishonor others."

When is the last time you found yourself in a conversation in the staffroom where someone was being dishonored? Unfortunately, the truthful answer to that statement might very well be "yesterday."

It happens *all the time*. It is so easy to get caught up in negative conversations about others, whether it is irritating colleagues, difficult students, or frustrating parents. There will always be another staff member with whom you do not see eye to eye; there will always be students who challenge your ability to love them and love your job; and these students behave this way because they have neglectful or self-seeking parents who have created these little monsters who seem to exist only to make your life miserable.

Make no mistake, teachers need to be able to converse with each other about the trials and tribulations they deal with on a daily basis. They need to vent, seek advice, and gain support from each other when they are struggling.

Yet regardless of how often you are "justified" in complaining about these colleagues, students, or parents, you will always have a choice to make when you initiate or find yourself in those types of conversations with colleagues. You can either conduct yourself with compassion and respect, ultimately seeking help or a solution to the challenge; or you can malign and dishonor those about whom you are speaking, and ultimately walk away from the conversation with no solution and feeling more negative than when it began.

It is a no-brainer to know which types of conversations will help you grow as a teacher and as a person, and which will not.

4. "It is not self-seeking."

The next verse also challenges teachers on a personal level not to use love in a way that is self-seeking. For example, have you ever had to tolerate a colleague going on and on about the sacrifices they made for the sake of the kids in their classroom? Listening to the hours they spent searching for modified lesson plans, the multiple contacts they made on behalf of a particular student, the extra time they spent before and after school helping students, and on and on, can be tiresome and frustrating and sometimes you would like to just shake that colleague and tell them "WE ALL DO THAT!"

Worse yet, have you been that colleague?

If you love your kids and make sacrifices for them, it is not necessary that everyone knows about your martyrdom. When teachers make sacrifices for kids only so that they receive recognition for their hard work, then obviously their motivation was not of pure intent.

5. "It is not easily angered, it keeps no record of wrongs."

This verse challenges teachers to wipe the slate clean every day. When educators truly love their job, they cannot allow themselves to be "easily angered," nor can they be justified in keeping a "record of wrongs." This is admittedly difficult, almost impossibly so.

There are so many possible obstacles in the path to achieving a perfect day: the messy and complicated lives that bring unpredictable issues when they walk through your classroom door; the complex and intricate relationships of the colleagues you meet in the hallways and chat with in the staffroom; and the system that makes decisions "in the best of interest of kids" that is confounding in its ineffectiveness because the people responsible for making the decisions might not have consulted those whom their decisions affect.

All of that, and the messiness and complexity of the teacher's personal life, and it is no wonder that the classroom is not a ticking time bomb for eruptions of emotions and, sometimes, anger. But if you allow yourself to get caught up in those negative emotions, and record each and every "wrongdoing" that you perceive was done to you in the memory bank of undeserved blame, you will lose your capacity to love your kids and love your job.

When you are filled with righteous anger over something someone said or did that you feel was a personal attack, it is impossible to make room for the more positive emotions that help a classroom flourish and help students succeed. And in the process, your own ability to flourish and succeed is likewise diminished. In short, no one wins when teachers are easily angered and keep a record of wrongs.

That is not to say that teachers should not stand up for themselves when they are wronged or stand up for others when they witness an injustice. By all means, advocate for what is right and just. The caution is not to hang onto the negative emotions in your crusade for righteousness, and not to get caught up in the petty garbage that distracts you from your purpose in the classroom.

Although it can be difficult to wipe the slate clean every morning and return to school after a challenging previous day, it is possible to do so if you view your perception of events through a positive lens. A dedicated and respected principle once commented on how she deals with the stress and frustration of being an administrator. She said that she does not believe for one second that people walk through the door of the school with the intent of doing their worst. She deliberately *chooses* to view every scenario with the belief that teachers, students, parents, or anyone who enters the school building do so with a desire to do their best for the sake of the kids.

Sometimes that desire gets waylaid by the daily grind of life, but it is there, buried within each person who walks through the school door. This principal's explanation is echoed in Indra Nooyi's (CEO of Pepsi) advice she learned from her father: "Whatever anybody says or does, assume *positive intent*. You will be amazed at how your whole approach to a person or problem becomes very different. When you assume negative intent, you are angry. If you take away that anger and assume positive intent, you will be amazed."

Assume the best of people. Assume they love their job, their school, their children as much as you do. And watch what happens when you reframe your perception to see people's actions with positive intent. This perspective will help you let go of the sense of being wronged and will help you let go of that list of wrongdoings to which you may keep adding, but rarely erase.

6. "Love does not delight in evil but rejoices with the truth."

It might not be apparent when you first read it, but there is a very fine line dividing the two parts to this verse. When you have been wronged, by a student, a colleague, a parent, an employer, whomever, you have options in how you react. It is very easy to "delight in evil," to sulk in self-righteous misery, feeling comforted and justified when others feed your anger by telling you how wronged you were. And when there are consequences enacted on the perpetrator of your hurt, well, even better! Revenge is sweet, right?

Wrong.

If you love your job and love your students, there is no room to dwell on anger and revenge, or to delight in evil. Any space given to those emotions takes away from the unconditional care your students need from you. They do not deserve your misplaced anger and frustration; they need your love. And the problem with wanting revenge and trying to defeat those who wronged us is that "it will test our faith, ethics, and morals, and leave us feeling empty even if we succeed in our efforts to beat our adversaries" (Coda and Jetter 2016, 113).

Choose to see life as an infinite array of choices. Every day, something will happen that you may not have asked for or chosen, but you still have the power to choose your reaction to it. No one can take that power away from you and it gives a sense of control over the uncontrollable situation in which you may find yourself.

This choice is an apt interpretation of this particular verse. When bad things happen in your teaching career, you can choose to delight in the evil surrounding the negativity by getting caught up in the angst, the need for revenge, and the temporarily satisfying reward of seeing someone brought to their knees for the harm they caused.

Or you can choose to rejoice with the truth. Even in the darkest moments of your career, this option is always available. The truth is this: you entered this profession knowing that it matters and believing that teachers can make a difference. That was the truth you started with, and it is the truth that will never fade. It can be easy to lose sight of that truth when you are feeling overwhelmed with whatever is going on in life that is dragging you down, but do not let go of the reason you applied to the College of Education in the first place. That truth is your hope and your joy. Rejoice in it.

7. "It always protects, always trusts, always hopes, always perseveres."

This is the kind of love educators are commissioned to be for the precious souls that grace the space between the four walls called the classroom. Teachers are commissioned to *protect* students from the evil in the world inasmuch as they have the control to do so in that space by respecting students' individuality and by teaching them to treat each other with that same respect.

Teachers are also sometimes obligated to *protect* students from a system and society that believe failure hurts rather than teaches. Compassionately allow students to make their mistakes and then hold them accountable to learning from them because otherwise when they leave these buildings of learning, they will not have learned some of the most important lessons that can be taught.

It is not just others from whom teachers have to try and protect their students, but also from themselves. Children and young adults can do themselves more damage than anyone could possibly do to them with their self-doubt and uncertainty. In showing students that they can expect great things of themselves by expecting it of them first, teachers are also teaching students that they are worthy of *trust*. And if teachers can *trust* students to work hard and achieve their potential, then they will likewise learn to *trust* themselves.

When kids learn to *trust* themselves, they understand there is *hope* for their future—a future to which they can meaningfully contribute because they have learned from their teacher that they have the abilities and skills to do so. Abilities and skills may come more naturally to some than others, but regardless of talent, these can be honed with conditioning and practice in a classroom where students are taught that effort and *perseverance* matter more than the gift of ability.

And this *perseverance* of achieving potential, begun in the classroom, is the quality that is going to shape these future citizens of every community into more than mere residents. They will become the next community leaders, minor sports coaches, volunteer board members, because they have been shown that their actions matter. In the classroom, they can learn that their dedication and commitment to *persevere* in support of a cause benefits the community of which they are a part. And they will gain the skill of tenacity because it was expected of them.

When kids have experienced the kind of love that protects them, trusts them, gives them hope, and perseveres steadfastly despite the challenges they face, then they can pass that kind of love on to the next generation.

And we all benefit.

8. "Love never fails."

There are two words in the English language that are used with such abandon that they have completely lost their meaning. *Always* and *never*. How many times have you heard kids complain "this class is so boring . . . it'll *never* end?!" (Ok, hopefully you actually have not heard kids say that!) Or how many times have you frustratingly commented to your child or your partner: "you are *always* on your phone!"

People use these words in hyperboles so often that when they are used in the sense for which they are intended, it is difficult to appreciate the depth and breadth of their meaning, and in failing to do so, it is impossible to appreciate their true significance.

Take a moment to ponder the true significance of the word *never* in this situation. Love *never* fails. *Never*. What does it look like if a teacher's love for their students and love for their job *never* fails? Educators can talk in theory about best teaching practices. They can philosophize about their values and the ideals they hope to pass on to their students. But in the day-to-day grind of lesson planning, marking, completing report cards, coaching, attending staff meetings, doing supervision, organizing field trips, disciplining, teaching, modeling, what does "love *never* fails" look like?

There are likely an infinite number of responses to this question, but there is one that is possibly the most effective, yet probably the most unheeded, because of its simplicity. Before this simple answer is offered, however, take a moment to frame your own response because this is the type of ambiguous question that can be answered correctly in multiple ways.

As you pause to consider what "love never fails" looks like in the daily routine of a classroom, consider your colleagues. Think about the co-worker you respect for the energy and enthusiasm they bring to their job every day. Reflect on the staff member whom the kids go to on their breaks, just to chat. Consider the teacher whose joy radiates in the staff room, and who avoids engaging in toxic conversations because they would rather not have that joy stifled or diminished.

What do those people all have in common? Do not make it complicated . . . keep it simple. What do you notice about those people who love their jobs and love the kids and for whom teaching is more than a job?

What you may have noticed is that the people whose love truly never fails for their kids and this profession cannot help but *smile*.

See? Simple. So simple, in fact, that it often goes unnoticed.

You may have answered this question with responses such as these teachers are at the school first in the morning and are the last to leave at the end of the day; their classrooms are inviting spaces with décor that reflects their passion for their subject area; they are always investing in their own growth by reading new professional development books and attending as many workshops as possible; they volunteer for every extra-curricular school event; they give up their own personal time to offer kids extra help; they spend hours planning new and interesting lessons; and the list could go on endlessly because there is no limit to what good teachers do who love their jobs.

While any and all of these answers are right and valid and absolutely demonstrate a sincere love for the profession of teaching, one of the greatest common denominators in each one of those amazing teachers is the simplicity of a genuine smile.

When students walk into the building in the morning and you happen to be greeting that day (which, by the way, is a necessary practice in which schools should engage, as kids should *always* be met at the door and welcomed by a staff member), what do the kids see? A teacher distracted by their phone, checking emails? Staff members too engrossed in each other's conversations to notice the kids coming through the doorway? Or are they greeted by a smiling adult who is prepared to welcome every individual child with the kindness and caring they need to understand that they are precious, beautiful, and valuable members of this place they call school?

After these students have entered through the front doors and have navigated the hallways, sometimes with wary trepidation for the unkind encounters that are an unfortunate reality in the school hallway, and arrive at their classroom doors, then what might they see? A teacher hurriedly finishing up marking? A teacher checking their text messages and social media? Maybe they do not even see a teacher because he or she has run to do some photocopying or grab a coffee.

While all of these are practical and excusable uses of a teacher's time (with the exception of social media!), what if teachers instead made a point of being at the door when the bell rings to welcome every student, with a smile, as they walk into the classroom? A senior biology teacher, Mr. H, does this each and every period of the day, without fail. He stands at his door, smiles, shakes each child's hand, and greets them by name as they pass into his classroom. There is no doubt that his students feel welcomed and valued as they enter that space.

In those small moments of welcome, relationships are built that will help see kids through the tough times in the class when concepts become hard, assignments are challenging, and life's stressors become overwhelming.

Kids *need* to start both their school day and every period throughout the day with that sense of welcome. For some, this moment of welcome is of much more importance than for others. The children who were sent from home with loving hugs and unconditional support will probably respond to your smile with one of their own and move on with their day, confident in their place in the school and their place in life.

But the children who barely made it to school because they spent the night on their own, or worse, spent the night avoiding abuse or taking care of the adult who should have been their caregiver—these kids may not smile back. There are too many weights on their shoulders and in their soul to allow for the lightness of upturned lips. But if these kids are greeted without fail every morning and every class thereafter by name and with a warm smile and genuine love, that consistency has the potential to register deep within. It sends a message that they *matter*, that someone *cares*, and that this place can offer something they might not get at home, a *love that never fails*.

> "And now these three remain: faith, hope and love. But the greatest of these is love."
>
> 1st Corinthians 13:13

How can educators even get through their day without relying on the concepts present in this verse? Teachers need *faith* to assure them that they are fulfilling their calling when the doubts assail, *hope* that they can be of use in service to the children who have been given to them to care for, and *love* for each beautiful soul that belongs in this world and in their classroom.

And if a teacher, the educated and mature adult in the room, needs the promise inherent in those three eternal truths, then how much more do the children in the desks need those same promises? They need teachers to show them how to have *faith* in themselves and their ability to reach their potential to contribute to the world. They need educators to teach them how to have *hope* that when they leave the classroom, they have the ability to grab hold of the possibilities that await them rather than fear the uncertainties of life. And lastly, they need to learn the power of the capacity to *love*—love for learning, and love and respect for others.

This is a huge and daunting task that teachers are called to fulfill. But when teachers diligently practice the values that they preach and make each of them a daily expectation of themselves and for their students, they have the power to turn the classroom into a place where learning curriculum is a pleasant by-product of the even more important lessons they can teach their students: lessons of respect, how to learn from their mistakes, and the value in serving others. Students of teachers who have intentionally used their classrooms to teach these kinds of lessons will be better equipped to make a positive difference in the world than those who have merely learned the content and skills presented in a textbook.

Chapter 14

Review and final exam

The review of each chapter is intended to help you prepare to reflect on the final exam questions at the end of each chapter summary.

1. Train up a Child

The "everyone gets a ribbon philosophy" has more potential for harm than good when it comes to children's education. Rather than celebrate mediocrity, schools should ascribe to the idea that students can achieve their potential through determined effort and intentional perseverance, and they should be rewarded for nothing less.

Angela Duckworth's research supports this belief by presenting indisputable evidence that demonstrates "without effort, your talent is nothing more than unmet potential. Without effort, your skill is nothing more than what you could have done but did not" (Duckworth 2016, 51). In applying this philosophy to the classroom, it is possible to find a balance between coddling kids too much and imposing impractically rigid standards. Through consistently encouraging and expecting perseverance, kids can be taught not to settle for less than their best but to believe in the assurance that effort is all that is required to reach their potential.

How do you train up children to achieve their potential in your classroom? If a new student walked into your class, how would their classmates describe you, your expectations of them, and your procedures for accountability?

2. Fall and Rise Again

It is easy to get caught up in the desire to protect students from harm, hurt, and failure, yet doing so comes at a cost. When children are not given the opportunity to fall and rise again, they cannot develop the characteristics of tenacity and grit that will help see them through the difficult times in life. Teachers' kind intentions of protecting students' feelings by reassuring them that their work is "good enough" and awarding them inflated marks might avoid the conflict of upset students and parents, but the long-term effects of this philosophy do more damage than good.

When teachers accept mediocrity rather than expect excellence, they are unintentionally reinforcing students' insecure beliefs that they cannot achieve any higher. Establishing systems of accountability in the classroom may initially frustrate students who have become complacent in their routines of "good enough," but when implemented with consistency and fairness, these systems of accountability teach students only to be satisfied if they have tried their best. Effective routines of expectation and accountability teach students how to rise when they fall, and that learning from the fall is better than being caught by a well-intentioned teacher.

What routines can you establish in your classroom that will help students learn to be accountable for their own learning?

3. Teach Yourself

Teachers already give so much of themselves that it may have been frustrating to read a chapter that asks you to give more. Yet if chapters 1 and 2 are dedicated to the belief that kids can, and will, reach their potential and exceed their own performance expectations when they are consistently and compassionately held to a high standard, then teachers cannot hypocritically expect any less of themselves.

If teachers expect the best from their kids, then they need to deliver their best to the students in their classrooms. And the truth is that a teacher's best cannot be achieved in a 9:00–3:30 school day. That might be the hours when a teacher gets to deliver their best; but there is no professional—athlete, musician, surgeon, lawyer—alive that can achieve excellence without a great deal of work and effort prior to the delivery of that performance.

Teaching should be, *must* be, no different from all other professions. Educators should hold themselves accountable to the same standards to which they vow to hold their students. They must model a passionate love for education that goes beyond the classroom boundaries in order to foster that same passion for learning in their students.

When you teach others, do you also teach yourself with the same expectations? How do your professional routines model the work ethic you expect of your students? Do students recognize that you value education and your time with them in the classroom?

4. Sharpen Each Other

Both sides of the collaboration versus competition debate could present resounding arguments that cite evidence for each being an effective instructional strategy. Yet perhaps the most effective strategy does not have to be one or the other but rather a combination of the two.

When students are engaged in learning through activities that require collaborative teamwork as they compete against their peers, their learning not only becomes authentic, it also becomes memorable and exciting. Competitive collaboration fosters conceptual discussions between students that simply do not occur when these opportunities are not provided. Not only are students more engaged in their learning with the types of theme-based lessons described in this chapter, but they are also more engaged with each other. The classroom becomes a learning experience in relationships and conflict resolution in addition to acquiring the skills of the course.

How can you encourage students to "sharpen each other" through lessons and activities that inspire healthy competition where students learn from, and challenge, one another? How can you turn mundane concepts into engaging games that provide students an end goal to strive to achieve?

5. Let Nature Teach You

If we are not careful, technology will become the "Frankenstein that destroys us," as Stegner predicted back in 1960. Providing students with the opportunity to experience nature, learn from it, and respect it, is one way to counter the all-consuming effects of technology in their lives. While not every teacher can engage with students in survival-type excursions, even short forays into the outdoors can stimulate students' creativity and foster reflection in ways that cannot be replicated within the four walls of a classroom.

Teaching outdoors is not only effective to provide students with authentic applications of the content they are studying, but it also provides the opportunity for them to experience some solo time away from the demands of their daily lives. In that solitude, they will experience the "geography of hope" that Stegner says only exists with an appreciation for the wilderness. Developing an awareness that they are part of a bigger world helps students put their problems and concerns into perspective and leaves them feeling hopeful and reassured.

How can you incorporate natural teaching into your routines so that your students learn to appreciate the world around them and to embrace the "geography of hope" that exists for the purpose of keeping people grounded? Do you have a place that is yours; a space that lends you a sense of peace and tranquility when the chaotic life of a teacher becomes overwhelming?

6. Turning Suffering to Hope

The reality of working with children and investing in them as people means that not only do teachers get to derive joy from their successes, but they are also inevitably hurt by students' sorrows. Kids come into your classroom and into your life with stories that would break the strongest of adults. These stories live out in a multitude of ways, depending on the child. They may lash out at their peers, making themselves unlikeable, or worse, they may try to force others to like them through their bullying tactics.

These children may deliberately try to make your life difficult through their disruptive and antagonizing behavior; and they may simply break your heart with their silence and unresponsiveness. Regardless of how their stories manifest themselves in the classroom, when you care about kids, you will hurt along with them.

This chapter dwells on what teachers can do when faced with a child who is hurting, and who is hurting others as a result of that pain. While teachers may not be able to change a student's life situation, they can be the constant source of love and encouragement that these kids may not experience anywhere but in the classroom.

How educators present themselves as that constant source may differ for every teacher, but what is important is the awareness that the simple things in life, like a cup of tea, can provide hurting students with the awareness that someone is willing to make time for them and that they are valuable enough to spend time with.

All students need this unconditional attention, but those who walk into your classrooms with stories that have the potential to break you; it is these students whose survival depends on it. Despite your concerted effort to supply that kind of time and attention, you may never actually gain their trust enough to hear their stories, but you will have shown them that there is another way to be, and that there is room for hope in the chaos of their lives.

Can you make time in your day to have tea with your students, time to simply listen without judgment, support without expectation, and care without reservation? What are the small things you do to help turn a child's suffering to hope?

7. Teach You Again

Regardless of where a teacher is on their professional journey, there is no educator who does not benefit from having their beliefs challenged and being pushed out of their comfort zone. Mentorship is often a practice reserved for new teachers coming into the profession, yet all educators can benefit from the mentorship experience. The necessary element in ensuring the mentorship relationship is successful and effective is the willingness of both participants to learn and grow from the experience.

Teachers who are willing to humble themselves and seek ways to develop their practice not only provide their students with a better learning experience, but they also model the value of lifelong learning.

Do you recognize that despite being a teacher yourself, you may need to be taught again? From whom can you seek help when you are bombarded with new subjects or grades for which you are unprepared to teach? Who can you turn to when you recognize you are drifting along the river of complacency and need to be challenged? How can you offer yourself in a mentorship capacity to others who are new to the profession or are struggling to see outside the comfortable box of their own making?

8. A Model of Good Works

There is little that might get your blood boiling more than the entitled behavior of children who have been raised and taught to expect that the world owes them a favor. This lesson, however, argues for the one thing to which all students are entitled from the moment they walk through the classroom door: respect.

The classic book *To Kill A Mockingbird* provides indisputable wisdom regarding this topic through the character of Atticus Finch, who sagely says "they are certainly entitled to think that, and they are entitled to full respect for their opinions" (Lee 1988, 139). This entitlement could, and should, become a classroom mantra, with one caveat. If students expect to be entitled to respect for their opinions, they must also demonstrate it to others.

Using the Quick Write practice from Penny Kittle's book *Write Beside Them*, you will see how students can be honest and vulnerable with themselves, with you, and ultimately with each other when respect is the dominant trait underlying every interaction. When students are willing to expose themselves, their thoughts, and their emotions in their writing, and then go so far as to share them with others, the powerful life lessons that are learned as a result are irreplaceable.

Is your classroom a space where children witness a model of good works? How do you ensure every child in your classroom is given the respect (by you and their peers) to which they are entitled? How many students in your class would feel comfortable sharing their thoughts or opinions on a sensitive topic? What can you do to increase that number of students?

9. Honor Everyone

Political allegiances are part of daily life. They exist in dissentious proclamations on social media and in tense conversations in social gatherings. These allegiances also exist in the classroom. Although the classroom should never be the place where teachers preach political indoctrination from a soapbox to a captive audience, it should be the place where students are taught to view issues from both left- and right- points of view. The classroom should be a space where students feel safe to share their views, but also where they are encouraged to challenge and critique the information presented to them by the media.

The classroom offers teachers the opportunity to preach and practice the democratic values upon which this country is built and therefore influence the next generation of citizens, voters, and politicians to continue a tradition of honor and respect for the democratic process—even when, *especially* when, they might disagree with the government's course of action.

Do you avoid political issues and topics in your classroom? How might you respectfully foster discussions regarding the political topics and issues that affect students' lives? What are some practical ways you can teach your students to critique and question information, yet in the meantime model how to honor others' points of view?

10. For the Rights of All

There is not a single teacher who does not have an opinion about how the system could be improved to better help kids. Educators work in a world where the system is structured and run by people who are often removed from the classroom and when they fail to consider the voice of those on the ground level, make mistakes that hurt teachers and hurt kids.

Ultimately, however, the frustrations teachers might experience with bureaucracy and politics that seem to hinder the work they can do with kids are an inevitable part of teaching. You may encounter situations where you are forced to recognize your own limitations and acknowledge that you cannot fix a system that is broken, nor can you prevent the powers of that system from hurting people. Yet rather than dwell on the brokenness of a system that you cannot control, seek instead ways that you can be a champion for kids. Speak out on behalf of those who cannot speak for themselves and fight with integrity the battles that are worth the fight. Regardless of the outcome of your advocacy, you will have shown someone you valued them enough to act on their behalf. That alone is a victory.

There is no greater gift than being made to feel worthy and valuable, and this is a gift that is in your power to give.

What are the flaws in your education system? Once compiled, critically examine your list and focus on one or two issues that have the most potential for negative consequences for kids. How can you advocate for kids in those circumstances? What actions can you take that will show your students they are worth fighting for?

11. Love Your Neighbor

How many students have gone through your building with the end goal of escaping not only the school itself, but the community in which they were raised? Consider making it a personal goal to help students not only see the good, and take pride, in their home community, but to *be* the good and the reason for pride.

Endeavor to find at least one way to either bring the community into the school or to take students out into the community in the courses you teach. This chapter provides a few specific examples of how this can be done in various courses that will hopefully spark your own imagination to build the bridge between the academic curriculum and your community.

And because school is more than an opportunity to teach kids "readin', writin', and 'rithmetic," some of the ways a school's Student Leadership Council connects the student body to the community are also provided.

The classroom you serve provides an opportunity to teach kids about service to others; and the entire community benefits when this lesson is taught.

Does your classroom encourage students to love your neighbor? Reflect on the outcomes and goals of the courses you teach. Brainstorm ways you could either take students out into the community, or have community members come into the school, to meet at least one outcome. Then take the next step and turn your brainstormed ideas into action.

12. When We Stumble

Considering the focus on others' mistakes in earlier chapters, such as exploring flaws in the system and how students can be taught to learn from their mistakes, this book would be remiss if it did not also provide an opportunity to reflect on how teachers' own flaws can cause stumbling blocks in the classroom. This lesson examines the necessity of teachers' ability, as professionals, to humble themselves and admit when they are wrong because doing so provides a comfortable space for children to do the same.

Do you create a space where mistakes are translated into learning opportunities by modeling humility yourself? Do students know that "when they stumble", they can learn how to rise again to become better, stronger, and more resilient because they have seen you do the same?

13. Faith, Hope, and Love

The popular Bible verse that is often used at weddings provides an intriguing lens through which to examine the teaching profession. Teaching is a test of faith, a perpetual vision of hope, and an unfailing love for the beautiful souls who grace the classroom. Regardless of your faith background, if you apply the wisdom of these verses to your daily lives in the classroom, kids benefit.

Teachers are better when they live out the faith that every single child is a beautiful creation worthy of love and capable of learning, and that their presence in the classroom is not a coincidence but part of a perfect plan. Teachers are better when they invite hope into the classroom, and into their interactions with children; a hope that dispels the fear that lingers and lurks in the hallway shadows. And indisputably, teachers are better when they can show their students in words and actions that they love their job because they love "their" kids.

Do you teach with faith, hope, and love at the core of all you do? Do you love your job and can others tell?

For They Preach, but They Do Not Practice

Students easily recognize the difference between teachers who commit to making their educational experiences memorable and those who are in the classroom merely for the paycheck and summer holidays. Students will learn to respect the teachers who model the values they preach and will learn to scoff at the hypocrisy of teachers who boast about, but fail to practice, those values.

Passion for teaching ignites passion for learning. When teachers model a love of education, a love for their profession, and a love for their students in all that they do, the classroom becomes an inspiring and safe place for students to rise to the challenge of achieving their potential.

What are the values on which you can build a foundation for your classroom? Do you actively live out those values?

Do you, in your daily interactions with students, *"practice what you preach"?*

Bibliography

Becker, M. (2016, April 5). 5 Benefits of Outdoor Education. Retrieved from Edutopia: https://www.edutopia.org/blog/5-benefits-of-outdoor-education-michael-becker.

Carrington, Jody. 2019. *Kids These Days: A Game Plan for (Re)Connecting.* Victoria: FriesenPress.

Coda, Rebecca, and Rick Jetter. 2016. *Escaping the School Leader's Dunk Dank: How to Prevail When Others Want to See You Drown.* San Diego: Dave Burgess Consulting, Inc.

Donne, John. n.d. "Discover Poetry." No Man Is An Island. https://discoverpoetry.com/poems/john-donne/no-man-is-an-island.

Duckworth, Angela. 2016. *Grit: The Power of Passion and Perseverance.* Toronto: HarperCollins.

Dweck, Carol. 2006. *Mindset: The New Psychology of Success.* Random House.

Echazarra, Alfonso. 2020. "Do students learn in co-operative or competitive environments?" *PISA in Focus.*

Gordon, Sherri. 2020. *Pros and Cons of Competition Among Kids and Teens.* September 17. Accessed September 29, 2021. https://www.verywellfamily.com/competition-among-kids-pros-and-cons-4177958.

Griffiths, Doug. 2011. *13 Ways to Kill Your Community.* Calgary: Frontenac House, Ltd.

Hess, Diana E., and Paula McAvoy. 2014. *The Political Classroom: Evidence and Ethics in Democratic Education.* New York: Routledge.

Kohn, Alfie. 1992. *No Contest: The Case Against Competition.* Boston: Houghton Mifflin.

Lee, Harper. 1988. *To Kill A Mockingbird.* New York: Grand Central Publishing.

Miker, Scott. n.d. "Scott Miker." https://www.scottmiker.com/improve-your-strengths.

Mill, John Stuart. 2019. John Stuart Mill: On Instruction, Intellectual Development, and Disciplined Learning. https://www.criticalthinking.org/pages/john-stuart-mill-on-instruction-intellectual-development-and-disciplined-learning/736#:~:text=and%20Disciplined%20Learning-,John%20Stuart%20Mill%3A%20On%20Instruction%2C%20Intellectual%20Development%2C%20and%20Discip.

Nesloney, Todd, and Adam Welcome. 2016. *Kids Deserve It!: Pushing Boundaries and Challenging Conventional Thinking*. San Diego: Dave Burgess Consulting, Ltd.

Oxford Languages. 2021. Oxford Languages. 10 13. Accessed 10 13, 2021. https://languages.oup.com/google-dictionary-en.

Sirota, Marcia. 2021. Dr. Sirota. Accessed 11 28, 2021. https://marciasirotamd.com.

Stegner, W. (1960, 12 3). The Wilderness Letter. Retrieved 10 14, 2020, from The Wilderness Society: https://www.wilderness.org/articles/article/wallace-stegner

Watson, Angela. 2019. *Fewer Things, Better*. Due Season Press and Educational Services.

Whitaker, Todd. 2013. *What Great Teachers Do Differently: 17 Things That Matter Most*. New York: Routledge.

Williams, J. J. (2017). School-based experiential outdoor education - A neglected necessity. Journal of Experiential Education, 58–71.

Zwaagstra, Michael C, Rodney A Clifton, and John C Long. 2010. *What's Wrong with Our Schools and How We Can Fix Them*. Plymouth: Rowman & Littlefield Education.

Acknowledgments

Thanks to my husband, Dave, who always provides an objective perspective and another way to look at a situation. Your logic and ability to see the big picture make me a better person.

Thanks to my kids, Marcail and Caleb. You are incredible people, unerringly created by a God who loves you and has blessed you beyond measure. I look forward to watching you use your gifts to make the world a better place.

Thank you to my parents. You were my first teachers, and I'm grateful that you have never abdicated that role when I still come to you for advice. Your modeling of hard work, grit, and grace have taught me to strive for the same.

Thanks to my mentors. Jim, your encouraging words of inspiration are always timely, whether they are early morning texts or wisdom offered in the heat of a ballgame. Bruce, your commitment to "fighting the good fight" taught me about loyalty and integrity. You are both the epitome of "practicing what you preach."

Thanks to my students. Your stories have shaped me, taught me, inspired me, and changed me. Thank you for trusting me with your stories and thank you for your willingness try something new every time I said, "I have an idea . . . !"

Thank you to my colleagues. In the ebbs and flows of my teaching career, I've had the opportunity to work with some amazing educators who daily live out the expectations they have for their students. That commitment to personal accountability is what sets you apart and it is the reason students admire and respect you. Thank you for being that teacher.

About the Author

Nicole Philp has a wide range of experiences in education, including teaching a variety of subjects and grades in both large urban and small rural schools. She has also worked as an instructional coach, co-taught an experiential outdoor school program, and was seconded to work as a consultant for the Ministry of Education in Saskatchewan, Canada. Awarded on provincial and national levels for her work with students, Nicole believes education provides the opportunity to teach lessons that go beyond the curriculum.